Sexual Abuse

Len Hedges-Goettl

EDITED BY DANIEL G. BAGBY

ABINGDON PRESS

NASHVILLE

SEXUAL ABUSE
PASTORAL RESPONSES

Copyright © 2004 by Abingdon Press

This book is printed on acid-free paper.

Library of Congress Cataloging-in-Publication Data

Hedges-Goettl, Len.
    Sexual abuse : pastoral responses / Len Hedges-Goettl ; edited by Daniel G. Bagby.
        p. cm.
    Includes bibliographical references.
    ISBN 0-687-04374-3 (paper adhesive : alk. paper)
    1. Sexually abused children—Pastoral counseling of. 2. Adult child sexual abuse victims—Pastoral counseling of. 3. Sexual abuse victims—Pastoral counseling of. I. Bagby, Daniel G. II. Title.

    BV4464.3.H42 2004
    261.8'3272—dc21

                                                          2003012038

04 05 06 07 08 09 10 11 12 13—10 9 8 7 6 5 4 3 2 1

MANUFACTURED IN THE UNITED STATES OF AMERICA

I would like to thank my wife, Barbara, and her mother, Jane Hedges, for their patience and watchful eyes throughout the process of writing this book. I would also like to thank my editor, Dr. Bagby, for his thoughtful responses to my work and the editorial staff at Abingdon Press for their patience with a new author.

This work is dedicated to the prevention of sexual abuse and is written as a solemn witness to the wounds of the victims.

Contents

Foreword

S exual abuse is a difficult subject, and talking about sexual abuse in the church is difficult. Helping parishioners and communities of faith deal redemptively with sexual abuse is an even greater challenge.

This second book in the Pastoral Responses series is again designed for pastors and other caregivers who minister to individuals and families through crises and significant difficulties. Like the first volume on addiction care, this contribution addresses a main concern in the human journey—the incidence of sexual irresponsibility. Called to offer advice, guidance, understanding, and comfort to parishioners and their families, caregivers must often deal with the medical, emotional, social, legal, and spiritual ramifications of sexual abuse.

Doctor Len Hedges-Goettl has provided an informative and useful resource for people in the parish who are trying to help people injured by sexual misconduct. Writing to pastors and lay ministers in the parish setting, this "practitioner of care" offers concrete, practical suggestions for caregivers facing the variety of challenges that sexual abuse brings to the local church and its members. The author invites readers to identify and understand sexual abuse, assists them in making distinctions between abuse and misconduct in regard to sexual matters, and explains the nature of sexual abuse and the most common myths associated with it. He then provides redemptive insights and responses for victims and abusers and suggests preventive steps for church, family, and individuals addressing the issue. With a genuine pastoral heart, he helps the reader understand the victim and minister to the victim and family and sets forth a blueprint for responsible ministry with the sexual abuser.

The volume is an ally in the delicate pastoral care of those who have been abused sexually.

Daniel G. Bagby, Ph.D.
Theodore F. Adams Professor of Pastoral Care
Baptist Theological Seminary at Richmond

Introduction: Leviathan

You have crushed Leviathan's heads*, gave him as food to the wild animals. (Psalm 74:14 NJB)

How many of us imagined we would be sitting together one morning listening to some pastor talk about sex?"

This is the opening question used for a seminar about the role and responsibility of worship communities with regard to abuse. The question is usually followed by some subdued nervous chuckles. The people in the room typically arrive braced for a difficult but important discussion, and they are grateful for an excuse to relax a little. Unfortunately the question serves as something more than an icebreaker. It is a sober reminder that a Leviathan of sorts has fully raised its ugly head and can no longer simply be ignored or covered up.

The popular press knows all too well that sex and scandal boost sales. Add a worship community to the mix, and you have the recipe for a story demanding national or even international attention. Like rubbernecks on the highway opposite a terrible accident, the reading public stops and attends when the report features sexual abuse and a church.

So now a title such as *Sexual Abuse: Pastoral Responses* is considered timely and important rather than just in bad taste. But this book was not written to capitalize on shocking

---

*Properly a mythical monster of chaos.

headlines. It is the result of years of work and research while wrestling with worship communities to stop denial and pay attention. The season of public scrutiny has been a long time coming and is not guaranteed to endure. Sexual abuse is like a hideous monster, with sex offenders as the monster's many claws. We now know the beast is real and can live in our own congregation. We understand now that, for those who are victims and for those who witness their testimonies, this chaotic monster can shake faith in our congregation. It may even shake the foundation of one's faith in God.

On any given Sunday, as a pastor greets the members of his small congregation, has he any idea how many of them bear the heartache and scars of sexual abuse? While working with yet another committee in her big-steeple church, does the senior pastor understand why some members seem bent upon inviting others to act abusively toward them, reenacting the abuse of their past? Sexual abuse survivors have not just begun to show up in our congregations, they have always been there. One nationwide telephone poll by *The Los Angeles Times* noted that 27 percent of women interviewed and 16 percent of men interviewed indicated that they were sexually abused when children.[1] Marie Fortune cites estimates of one in three girls and one in eleven boys suffer sexual abuse.[2] In *Father-Daughter Incest,* Judith Herman reports that her clients include significant percentages of Catholics, Protestants, and Jews, meaning that even in a congregation numbering as few as seventy-five people, twenty to twenty-five women and six to thirteen men have likely been sexually abused.[3] And these figures only account for persons who were sexually abused as children, saying nothing about those whose abuse happened when they were adults. Further, unlike physical abuse, of which more cases are reported among the poor and disenfranchised, I know of no substantive evidence to suggest the same is true for sexual abuse.[4] Indeed, clinical experience demonstrates that all congregations, rural to urban, with steeples tall to small, have those among us who are scarred by sexual abuse.

Left alone, victims, abusers, and their families can follow a path of failure and destruction of themselves and others. Therapy can help, but therapy alone does not serve to heal and minister to the damaged and disfigured spiritual selves of everyone involved.

Discussing sexual abuse in conjunction with other forms of abuse, the U.S. Advisory Board on Child Abuse and Neglect declared the problem *a national emergency* in their 1990 publication and specifically asked religious institutions to join as part of the solution in their 1991 publication, writing:

> The Board believes that, because of their broad base and deep historic roots, as well as their accessibility to children, family, neighborhood, and community, religious institutions often possess a unique capacity to initiate those activities necessary for the promotion of a responsive community child protection system. Moreover, where necessary, they are often able to foster the accountability of that system. . . . Responsibility for solving the complex problem of child maltreatment cannot be placed at the doorstep of the nation's religious institutions. Still, the Board believes that—because they have been, and will continue to be, an integral part of neighborhood and community life—their potential as agents of positive change in connection with child maltreatment needs to be tapped more effectively.[5]

Worship communities are distinct from other sources of healing and relationship and can fulfill a unique role. Pastors, like therapists, build trust-based relationships; but unlike therapists, pastors concern themselves with the spiritual well-being of those they serve. Further, pastors often establish trust-based relationships with members based upon the members' healthy desires for spiritual growth. Establishing this relationship of trust around concerns for health and wholeness (rather than basing the relationship first upon healing a sickness, as with therapists), pastors have unique and sustained influence through the lives of the members.

Studies of therapeutic efficacy have shown that instilling hope is an essential component in the healing process.[6] As long as there has been pastoral concern, the assurance of hope has been a primary tool.

> In Judaism, as early as the first three chapters of Genesis the central issues of pastoral care are evident: God's creativity and help; human potential and brokenness; family alienation and the promise of reconciliation; and *the persistence of hope* even in the face of despair and death.[7]

But many pastors remain understandably afraid to tackle an issue as sensitive as sexual abuse. Most of us feel ill prepared, and many of us carry our own history of sexual encounters that may invite us simply to leave the matter to other, better-suited helpers. Feeling uneasy about sexual issues among professionals is not unique to pastors. Recently, in consultation with another therapist regarding the inappropriate sexual behavior of a child, a therapist found it difficult to say the word "masturbation," much less to discuss frankly the child's sexual history. And truly, all these concerns have some foundation. Some pastors do not avoid addressing sexual behavior but may unwittingly do so in a manner that contributes to the pain and alienation that fuels the problem. But more often the *silence* of one in a ministry of compassion to a victim or an abuser *reinforces the lie* that sexual abuse is a shameful *secret* that must stay forever unspoken and be borne in silence.

Sexual abuse is a chaotic monster that damages the image of God and denies incarnation in victims, abusers, and even in those closest to them. Spiritual wholeness, including "sexual shalom," is mocked as trust and hope are systematically destroyed. But the psalmist promises that God can crush the Leviathan's heads! This resource seeks to equip pastors, educators, spiritual directors, and anyone called to a ministry of compassion to begin to address this hurt.

As one reads this book, several cautions, all concerning self-care, are extended. For anyone, frank discussion of sexual abuse is a disquieting experience. If one believes that she or he can treat the violation of others completely dispassionately, that person is likely cut off from his or her emotional and psychological life to an unhealthy extent. This topic is a hard one. Although every attempt is made to avoid unnecessarily graphic descriptions, the topic alone invokes stress. For anyone whose history includes maltreatment, even if it was not sexual maltreatment, this resource will likely stir up old memories and unresolved hurts. Please be aware of yourself as you read this book. Many a stoic Christian has told me that "we all have our cross to bear," suggesting that one should simply shut up and put up with his or her own "cross." I often remind helping professionals that even Jesus did not bear his cross alone. Please do not bear this cross alone; monitor your own response as you read, and speak with others you trust. If you find more to bear in yourself than you expected, seek a trained counselor and be open to pastoral care.

Finally, let me say something about this book's organization. The first chapter seeks to share the vocabulary and a context for the discussion. Although not clinically exhaustive, it seeks to provide a framework for approaching a multidimensional problem. The second chapter is essential if we are to understand the variety of motivations and behaviors that can result in sexual abuse. If sexual abuse is viewed as a monolithic problem, prevention and response efforts would likely be too narrow to meet the needs. Nevertheless, reading about abusers typically raises great anxiety, so a chapter addressing some strategies to address the problem concretely is next. In the third chapter, practical suggestions for prevention are given, and several aspects of a sexual misconduct policy are enumerated. With a calmer head, the reader is then invited to consider several dimensions of personality and behavior in victims in chapter 4. The fifth chapter addresses ministry opportunities to avoid inadvertent harm to victims and to assist in the spiritual healing and reconciliation for everyone involved.

1

The Nature of Sexual Abuse

How long will you love vain words, and seek after lies?
But know that the LORD has set apart the faithful for himself;
the LORD hears when I call to him. (Psalm 4:2-3)

NATIONAL ATTENTION: WHY NOW?

If church staff are to understand the *nature* of the problem of sexual abuse and to address it within their own worship communities, they would do well to understand why the problem has been actively avoided for so long. They may also understand any current resistance as they try to address the problem now.

Then

It was the late 1980s when televangelists became caricatures for philandering cheats, although, of course, few mentioned the abusive aspects of the situation. Instead, the moral implications of a sinful "holy man" were emphasized. At that time, I spent one year of seminary internship with sexual abuse survivors. A local congregation in Princeton opened its basement for weekly meetings. Posters appeared in some churches, but one congregation refused to allow the poster, saying, "We don't have people like that here." It is the fondest fantasy of every congregation that "those people"—

victims or victimizers—do not live in their community. But the posters went up, and even Princeton had enough victims to make a group.

During that internship, I organized a statewide conference for leaders, staff members, and educators in synagogues and churches throughout New Jersey. Literally hundreds of worship communities were notified by mail. Marie Marshall Fortune, the author of a new book about clergy abuse, agreed to be the keynote speaker.[1] After months of careful planning and hours spent advertising the event, the seminar was canceled due to lack of enrollment.

Recently

The media furor of 2002 and the special meeting between the Pope and high-ranking American Catholic clergy led to a new, controversial U.S. policy for Roman Catholic congregations with near zero tolerance of sex-offending priests.[2] The 214th General Assembly of the Presbyterian Church (USA) passed a resolution with several important components in 2002. The resolution urges all officers of the PCUSA to act as if they are "mandated reporters" (more on that in chapter 3); counsels governing bodies to refuse to enter into confidential agreements, sealed settlements, or "alternative resolutions" that keep secret credible allegations of sexual misconduct with minors; instructs PCUSA governing bodies to make known any current agreements by which child sexual offenders may remain a danger to children; and makes other judicially based recommendations.[3] How could so much change in the course of twenty years?

One premise suggests the problem of sexual abuse has only recently reached the dimensions that demand widespread public scrutiny. Unfortunately, historic data (including biblical accounts) do not support this notion.[4]

Instead of a "new problem" that reflects how terrible things have become in our world today, sexual abuse is a problem as old as time. Our attention to it may actually be a reflection of how much better (in some respects) things are today.

A Brief History

A sad truth, documented so often that it is nearly axiomatic, is that even counting the numerous adult women who are abused (most often by men who are known to them), the preponderance of sexual abuse victims are children (including teenaged children). Several resources recount the history of child maltreatment since antiquity.[5] As the *role* of children changed throughout the centuries, public scrutiny of their treatment increased and maltreatment was no longer tolerated. Rather than recount the explicit history of maltreatment here, the short outline below (discussed in more length in the resources cited later) suggests the slow change in the role of children over the centuries, which finally resulted in our attention to their sexual abuse.

Century	Status of Children	Notable Documents/Events
Antiquity	Equal to inanimate objects	700 B.C.E.—*Patria Potestas* law: Father's supreme right to sell, mutilate, or destroy his children.
1st century C.E.	Nearly equal to animals	*Gynaecology* published: suggesting "selective" infanticide.
2nd–15th	Trained like animals	From Plutarch to Pepys, including the "Christian" remembrance of "Innocents' Day," public whipping.
16th	Economic resource	Doctrine of *laborare es orare:* Work is worship versus Rousseau—"Speak less of the duties of children and more of their rights."

Century	Status of Children	Notable Documents/Events
18th–19th	Humans with rights (but economic burden)	Laws regarding child labor and corporal punishment.
19th	Emotional asset to be valued	Nuclear family promotes privacy; Society for the Prevention of Cruelty to Animals files the first suit on behalf of an abused child —1873
20th	Persons to be protected	1906—Thomas Rotch uses X rays to document abuse; 1962—C. Henry Kempe discusses "The Battered Child Syndrome"; 1974—National Center for Child Abuse and Neglect (NCCAN) begun; 1980—Child Welfare Act

The chart above chronicles the improved status of children and increased scrutiny of their treatment. But one does well to note that before the 1980s, little attention had yet been paid to sexual abuse.

Finally, in 1979, D. Finkelhor published *Sexually Victimized Children*,[6] and J. Fay published *He Told Me Not to Tell*.[7] These early publications signaled the beginning of public attention to child sexual abuse and were followed by F. Rush's book, *The Best Kept Secret: Sexual Abuse of Children*[8]; J. Herman's *Father-Daughter Incest*[9]; *I Never Told Anyone: Writing by Women Survivors of Sexual Child Abuse*, edited by E. Bass and L. Thornton[10]; and *Sexual*

Violence: The Unmentionable Sin by the Reverend M. Fortune.[11]

At last, child sexual abuse was not entirely ignored. But even though it was not ignored, the discussion was not well received. As an example, the recently released exposé by Bruni and Burkett, *A Gospel of Shame,* that highlights the problem of clergy sexual abuse was originally published in 1993 but went out of print until its redistribution in 2002, in the face of public outrage at press reports.[12]

The change in the role of children and growing intolerance of their maltreatment set the stage to address sexual abuse. However, the publication of the frank discussions of the problem of sexual abuse, combined with pressing financial and legal concerns (see chapter 3), have ultimately ended denial of the problem, even in churches, for the time being.

Just because more of us are willing to talk about the problem now does not make overcoming centuries of denial and "turning of a blind eye" trivial. The improved status of children and increased public scrutiny of their treatment served to shed some light on the problem, but social myths (see chapter 2) continue to subdue frank conversation addressing sexual abuse.

CATEGORIES OF SEXUAL BEHAVIOR AND TYPES OF SEXUAL ABUSE

abuse, v.t.,

1. to use ill; to maltreat; to misuse; to use with bad motives or to wrong purposes; as to *abuse* rights or privileges.
2. to violate; to defile.[13]

The charge of sexual abuse is very grave, suggesting the second rather than the first of the definitions used above. There is no categorically accepted definition of which inappropriate sexual behaviors constitute abuse. In fact, there is not a clinical definition for what distinguishes sexual abuse from other inappropriate sexual behaviors anywhere in the *Diagnostic and Statistical Manual of Mental Disorders, Fourth Edition (DSM-IV),*[14] although the manual does provide a code for treatment when the focus of clinical attention is sexual abuse of either a child (V61.21) or an adult (V61.1).

The problem of defining sexual abuse is not simply an academic one. Definitions affect every aspect of the lives of the alleged abuser and the alleged victim. For an alleged abuser, it can mean the difference between conviction for a crime and individual liberty. For a victim, it can mean the difference between feeling silenced or without words to describe what happened and being heard.

A Confusing Situation

Marie[15] is a sophomore attending the local college and has attended your church for most of the semester. She comes to Bible study, helps out with church dinners, and enjoys extended conversations following worship. Last Sunday, she made an appointment to meet with you to discuss a private matter that has been troubling her for a long time. When she arrives at your office, she asks if you can keep what she says in absolute confidence. You assure her that as long as there is no immediate danger to anyone (see chapter 5), and since she is an adult, you can promise absolute privacy. She tells you that ever since she went through puberty, her father has made blatant sexual remarks about her and her appearance (for example, "Honey, you are very sexy in that dress, and I don't mean that in a fatherly way."). Although he has never touched her inappropriately or threatened to violate her sexually, he secretly continues the practice of making these remarks. Marie is currently seeing a therapist, but she is uncomfortable calling what happened to her "abuse." How can you begin to help Marie by giving her acceptable words to talk about what has happened to her?

Concentric Circles

Knowing the old axiom about the worth of pictures, let us consider two diagrams that help give words to a complicated set of behaviors.

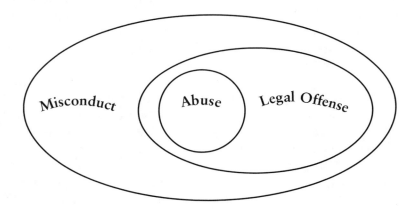

Nature of the Behavior

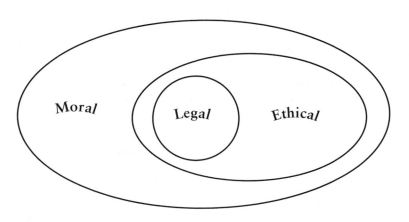

Type of Behavioral Breach

There is no excuse for inappropriate sexual behavior in any circumstance. But to classify all inappropriate sexual behavior as abuse may be both confusing and dishonest. It really does not help a person such as Marie to tell her that she has been sexually abused, especially when she understands her experience to be something other than *sexually* abusive. On the other hand, giving Marie appropriate words to describe her experience helps her have a vocabulary so she can talk about it without excusing or minimizing her father's behavior.

Consider the "nature of the behavior" illustrated above. While one may argue that all sexual abuse is against the law (the abuse circle is entirely inside the offense circle), not all illegal sexual behavior constitutes abuse. Illegal sexual behaviors include contact and noncontact sex offenses. I know of no contact sex offenses (rape, sexual assault, incest, child sexual contact, and so on) that are not also abusive. There are, however, noncontact sex offenses that one might argue do not always constitute sexual abuse. Examples of noncontact illegal sex offenses that may not be abusive to others include voyeurism (being a Peeping Tom) and public masturbation. Noncontact sex offenses can be psychologically damaging to the victim (hence *emotionally* abusive) and are always wrong but may not sexually violate or defile the victim. Hence they are not *always* sexually abusive. These statements can be very controversial until one works with victims who often struggle to understand and name the damage done to them. Victimization of any kind is so abhorrent that victims typically incorporate the experience into their lives from then on. Often, for the victim, calling an experience "sexual abuse" means something important for how they will define themselves in the future. Therefore the label should not be assigned lightly. In healing situations, the term "sexual abuse" should probably not be assigned by anyone except the victim.

A further step outside the "nature of behavior" circle concerns sexual misconduct. Although sexual misconduct (such as the sexual harassment experienced by Marie) may not be illegal, it is nevertheless psychologically damaging (and emotionally abusive). Calling the behavior "misconduct" allows both the victim and the perpetrator to acknowledge the behavior as categorically wrong without arguing about labelling it as sexual abuse. Further, calling the behavior "sexual misconduct" allows professional organizations (corporate entities or the Department of Human Services) to take action against the behavior if it occurs on the job or in families, even though the behavior is not legally a sex offense.

It may also be helpful to consider the type of behavioral breach (the nature of the violation) experienced because of inappropriate sexual behavior. Although a breach of laws allows victims to press charges against abusers, there can be ethical (professional) breaches that may not break a law (such as sexual harassment) but can result in job-related actions. Ethical violations can only be prosecuted in professional situations, however, and do not provide recourse in most family or informal situations. Finally (as in Marie's case), some actions may not be a clear breach of established laws or codes of ethics but are a breach of morality nonetheless. It is in these cases that religious communities can offer support and affirm the wrong done to victims even if other official agencies pragmatically may not. Churches fill a unique role in society by discussing publicly the boundaries of moral behavior.

SEXUAL ABUSE CATEGORIES

Categorizing by the Nature of the Act

When confining ourselves to sexual *abuse*, there are several ways of categorizing the problem. For example, inappropriate sexual behavior can be categorized by the *nature of the act* as either *contact* or *noncontact* sexual abuse.

It may surprise some readers to discover that some noncontact behaviors are abusive to others. A clear example would be the production and distribution of child pornography. Given the universal assumption that children cannot give their consent to sexual activity, child pornography exploits nonconsenting victims and damages them sexually (especially as it violates their sexual privacy and forces the destruction of appropriate sexual boundaries). Likewise, the distribution of any pornographic images to minors both violates acceptable sexual boundaries and defiles their normal path of sexual development. (To any reader wishing to "normalize" the practice by teenage boys of ogling "soft-porn" magazines, I would direct the critic's attention to the normal sexual development of children for centuries prior to having access to such material.) The precocious sexual development of children need not be accepted as a new societal norm, and the boundaries of moral behavior can be delineated.

Sexually abusive *contact* behaviors can be further divided according to the ages of the abuser and the victim. Specifically, contact sexual abuse includes adult-to-adult, adult-to-child, and child-to-child abuse.

Adult-to-adult sexual abuse includes the rape or sexual assault of a nonconsenting adult. Date rape, spousal sexual abuse, sexual molestation, and coerced sex between adults fall within this category.

Adult-to-child abuse can be further divided into two categories. *Pedophilia* describes a persistent sexual attraction (and inappropriate sexual behavior) toward young children who are not yet pubescent (typically younger than age thirteen). When attraction and contact is concentrated on pubescent children (ages thirteen through eighteen), the term used is *ephebophilia*.[16] Although both behaviors constitute child sexual abuse, the pattern of attraction in the abuser is significantly different (see chapter 2).

Child-to-child abuse can and does occur. To the victim, this abuse is just as devastating as sexual abuse from an adult. The significant difference is that the abuser, especially when prepubescent, is often acting out of his or her own experience as a sexual abuse victim and may have a different motivation than some adult abusers. The prognosis for treatment of the abuser in these cases may be better than for adult pedophiles. Further, efforts at sexual abuse prevention can fall short if the reality of child-to-child sexual abuse is not recognized. Finally, to react to a child offender strictly as an abuser, without exploring what produced his or her sexually precocious behavior, may result in the continued abuse by the person who sexually abused the child offender.

Categorizing by Relational Status

A different approach is to categorize sexual abuse according to the *relational status* of an abuser and the victim. The relative power of each person and the limits of physical boundaries vary according to the relational status (that is, different between a husband and wife than a parent and child or a pastor and congregant) but are essential elements of any relationship. Sexual abuse emphasizes a *power differential* (that is, situations in which the abuser either has more power than the victim or has power over the victim), including a physical power differential, as with rape, or a social power differential, as with coerced sexual relationships between a boss and an employee. Sexual abuse can also emphasize *a violation of appropriate intimate boundaries,* as with incest.

Sexual abuse by adult offenders always includes a power differential and often includes (or is about) violence. Rape is always, fundamentally, a violent rather than a sexual act. Some special cases of sexual abuse by adults, however (for example, when the adult offender has either mental retardation or a severe mental illness), may not be primarily about violence but still exploit a power differential. Some sexual abuse by adults, in which an appropriate intimate boundary (or covenant relationship) is violated, may or may not be primarily a violent act (see the discussion about diminished capacity to consent below) but always exploits a power differential. Likewise, sexual abuse of children *by* children may or may not be primarily an act of violence but always exploits a power differential.

Clergy sexual abuse both exploits a power differential and violates an intimate boundary (or covenant relationship). As clergy, many victims imbue the abuser with exceptional (even spiritual) power that cannot be resisted. Also, being clergy implies a "covenant relationship" (a relationship based upon a promise—one's ordination vows) with those the clergy serves. Sexual violation breaks the covenant and violates the "promised" boundary that exists between clergy and those they serve. Like incest, clergy sexual abuse is a "double" violation.

Diminished Capacity to Consent, Forced Consent, and Dual Relationships

Boundaries to sexual behavior in relationships are not always clearly defined. One's capacity to consent to sex, the right to withhold consent, and the complications of "dual relationships" can all be gray areas for determining whether the behavior is abusive.

A religious leader may violate appropriate sexual boundaries with the apparent consent of the other person, but that person may have a *diminished capacity* to give genuine consent because of his or her life circumstance. If a congregant is distraught and finds comfort; is inordinately awed by the religious leader's position, role, or status; credits the religious leader for helping him or her achieve some ecstatic experience of spirituality; is emotionally or mentally unstable while meeting with clergy, the congregation member may have a *diminished capacity* truly to consent to sex with the religious leader.

Religious leaders, by virtue of their position, role, and status, hold the greater responsibility for maintaining appropriate sexual boundaries even if a congregant invites the leader to violate those boundaries. As leaders, they have power and authority, whether they want that to be the case or not. With

2 8

power and authority come greater responsibilities. Having a sexual relationship with a congregant may be more than immoral, it may be abusive.

Diminished capacity to consent may also arise in dating relationships when participants use intoxicating substances (drugs or alcohol). Diminished capacity to consent may also be at issue when either participant has mental illness or significant cognitive impairment. Whenever the capacity to consent is significantly diminished, sexual behavior might be abusive.

Sexual relations between married persons may also fall within a gray area since some people doubt a spouse's right to withhold consent to sex. Although spouses have been convicted of rape by United States courts, historic theological notions of "conjugal covenant" can be confusing, or even damaging, to spouses who feel forced to consent to sex in order to remain "faithful to their marriage vows."[17]

A final gray area involves situations in which dual relationships exist. A pastor who dates a current congregant has two relationships with the congregant: pastor and paramour. Sex between these adults (albeit immoral if they are not married) may not necessarily be abusive. However, the difference in power and the nature of the pastoral relationship between pastor and congregant are confused when they are also dating. What does the dual relationship communicate to others whose pastoral relationships do not include this level of attraction? What may be inferred (even if unfounded) about the pastor's use of pastoral influence in this dual relationship? Another troubling dual relationship might involve a pastor who dates the student pastor intern or a staff member whom the pastor supervises. In general, avoid dual relationships if possible; they create unnecessary difficulties.

A good rule of thumb for pastors could be to forgo all intimate relationships with congregants for a reasonable period after the dual relationship has ended (similar to the ethical principles for psychologists). This rule would require the pastor or the pastor's paramour to change congregations and to abstain from intimate relations until after the dual relationship has clearly ended.

TECHNOLOGY AND THE FUTURE
OF SEXUAL ABUSE

For adult and child victims alike, most sexual abusers are known to them or even are a part of their own families.[18] Recently, however, inappropriate uses of the Internet have threatened to add a new category to the future of sexual abuse.

We should be clear that there are many documented benefits to the appropriate use of the Internet, including: the creation of "grassroots electronic communities,"[19] better students,[20] and even increased communications with missing children.[21] But, as Dr. Janet Stanley points out, when used inappropriately, the Internet also provides "increased opportunities for the solicitation of children and the committing of abusive acts by offenders outside the family."[22]

For children, the problem is large and growing. U.S. convictions for online offenses against children are over 1,000 and rising.[23] In an era in which as many as 63 percent of all children interviewed in the United States (age nine to seventeen) claim to prefer using the Internet to watching T.V.,[24] as many as 19 percent of child Internet users (age ten to seventeen) claim they are "approached" for sex at least once a year.[25] Of those, only 25 percent told a parent and only 10 percent approached the police because of the incident.

Studies have demonstrated that the Internet is used to advertise for "child sex tourists"[26] and now includes 23,000 sites and 40,000 chatrooms that defend adult-to-child sexual relations.[27] Pornographic sites have been estimated at 14 million,[28] with an estimated 1 million pornographic images of children.[29]

The threat of sexual abuse from inappropriate use of the Internet is certainly not restricted to children. Consider the warning to adults found in *The Internet for Dummies:*

Many people in chat groups lie about their occupation, age, locality, and, yes, even gender. Some think that they're just being cute, some are exploring their own fantasies, and some are really sick. . . . If you're a grown-up and choose to meet an online friend in person, use at least the same caution that you would use in meeting someone through a newspaper ad.[30]

Fortunately, the advent of this new category for sexual abuse has not gone entirely unnoticed. On October 30, 1998, Public Law No: 105-314 was signed by the President of the United States.[31] The law, called the "Protection of Children from Sexual Predators Act of 1998," includes provisions to punish those who produce or traffic child pornography through the Internet or who use the Internet to sexually offend against children or who transfer obscene material to minors by the Internet. In 1999, about three hundred child care and child protection specialists, Internet specialists and service providers, media practitioners, law enforcement agencies, and government representatives met at the U.N.-affiliated UNESCO headquarters in Paris and issued a declaration and action plan.[32] In response, persons from twenty-eight countries formed "Innocence en Danger," a nonprofit association in France that pursues the objectives of the UNESCO action plan.[33]

Besides the obvious benefit to efforts at sexual abuse prevention, knowledge about sexual misconduct by using the Internet also calls attention to security concerns for churches that have computers with Internet capabilities on-site. Recently, an Episcopal priest was charged with breaking the law cited above with the computer located in his church office.

CONTEXT, DEFINITIONS, AND CATEGORIES

This chapter sought to identify a part of the social context in which sexual abuse has come to the forefront of national attention. Likewise, some language was provided to talk about the problem and to distinguish abuse from other sexually inappropriate behaviors. Finally, some categories of sexual abuse were described to allow for a more nuanced discussion. Using the context, definitions, and categories as a "common lexicon," one can further explore the problem of sexual abuse and the unique pastoral role of the church in response to the problem.

2

Myths and Facts About Sexual Abuse and Sex Offenders

The simple believe everything,
but the clever consider their steps. (Proverbs 14:15)

It's seven in the morning and the telephone screams for attention. It's a staff worker from your congregation, and she hasn't slept all night. Late last night a teenage boy from your church told her he was having sex with an adult church worker. What should she do? Her boss told her to "investigate" more while he speaks to a lawyer. But the boy is leaving the country soon on a church-sponsored mission trip, and shouldn't she report this to somebody? Should you report it? Couldn't there be trouble if it is not reported soon? But what if it is a false allegation? Besides, if the boy is like others his age, didn't he just get what he wanted? How can we call this abuse? It all seems so complicated.

A Sunday school teacher is embarrassed and afraid. One of the girls in her class told her that her father was forcing her to do sexual things. No one ever told her what to do in a case like this. The teacher has just established a new relationship with this family. Should she work with the family and try to resolve this issue? If she speaks about the abuse, will it make the child less safe? Maybe she should tell the girl to talk about it with her mother—"After all, it's about [whispered] *sex!*"

Both prevention efforts and our pastoral response to sexual abuse have a direct effect on the lives and vocations of real people. We truly face a case of "what we don't know *can* hurt us (or someone else)." It is not acceptable to expose potential victims to increased risk or to allow revictimization because of our ignorance. Neither is it acceptable to deny important ministry opportunities to people of good faith because of false assumptions or unfounded allegations. The balance between preserving safety, on the one hand, and avoiding a witch hunt, on the other, can only be struck when we carefully evaluate what we know versus what we *think* we know.

With respect to sexual abuse and sex offenders, some facts are known, but few absolute conclusions can be drawn. Fortunately, several facts serve to dispel previous assumptions that heretofore threatened the safety of potential victims or falsely implicated whole groups as potential offenders. Oddly, knowing what is *not* true (acknowledging myths or false assumptions) may prove to be as important as learning some discrete facts.

SOME COMMON MYTHS

The myths concerning sexual abuse, victims, and offenders can create an environment in which well-meaning responses can make the problem worse instead of better. Unfortunately, some of us make a good-faith effort to do what is right without carefully examining the underlying assumptions we hold and that drive what we do or say.

The following is a brief discussion of some of those myths or false assumptions and how they may affect us. They are not listed in any particular order. This list represents some of the most common myths heard during church seminars and elsewhere about sexual abuse.

Myth 1: Sex Is Bad

There is a long tradition of celibate religious communities throughout history and across various religious traditions.

34

Early American Puritan history especially is replete with examples of celibacy being celebrated, and at times elevated and sanctified. In the United States' Christian traditions, both Protestant and Catholic examples of celibate communities are evident, from Shakers to priests.

Among some celibate sects, avoiding sexual behavior marked efforts at increased holiness.[1] Unfortunately, these efforts may suggest that there is something "unholy" about engaging in sex. Indeed, ascetic notions of the denial of pleasure to attain holiness may strongly invite one to believe that sex is bad.

Some Christian denominations have been very careful to identify celibacy as a "gift" that in no way diminishes the "gift" of human sexuality. But the manner in which the gift of human sexuality is discussed (or avoided) in religious communities may cause members to doubt that sex is a good thing. Further, discussion of which sexual behaviors are morally acceptable or morally unacceptable (such as sex only with the potential for procreation, prohibitions against homosexual sex and masturbation, and so on) may lead an uninformed listener to conclude that even though sex is *necessary* to continue our species, it is also really "naughty."

Celibacy can be a gift or a spiritual discipline to which some are called by God. But it is hardly controversial anymore to admit that sex, in and of itself, is not bad. Morality demands that one scrutinize the *circumstances* and *situations* related to any normal behavior, including sex, to determine if the behavior is appropriate or "good." But like many human behaviors, the act of sex in and of itself is not bad.

The myth of sex as bad may not be a conscious message we communicate directly but may be propagated every time sex is discussed in whispers or with great embarrassment. If sex could be considered "intimate" rather than "bad," the myth would not be supported. But when sex is something dirty or disgusting, rather than intimate, then silence about sex becomes the norm.

When one considers the problem of sexual abuse specifically, one may easily recognize that secrecy is paramount for the abuser to continue the abuse. If sex is thought of as bad or dirty or disgusting, then it becomes easier for the abuser to convince the victim to remain silent. Further, the victim is imbued with shame just for being the victim of an act thought inherently bad. This shame may occur whether or not the victim experienced certain aspects of the sexual abuse as pleasurable (an unfortunate possibility in some cases). Victims commonly claim shame because the act was sexual and often decide that since sex is bad, dirty, or disgusting, they likewise are bad and dirty and disgusting.

Myth 2: Sex Is Good

American culture's history of the celebration of sex in the "sexual revolution" invites some people to overreact to the myth of sex as bad by declaring *all* sexual behavior to be categorically good. This overreaction leads to organizations that promote exploitative or abusive sexual behavior (for example, C.O.Y.O.T.E. [Call Off Your Old Tired Ethics], a union for "legal" prostitutes in Nevada; or N.A.M.B.L.A. [North American Man-Boy Love Association], a group that promotes homosexual pedophilia as "good" or "healthy").[2]

Like the myth that sex is inherently bad, the myth that it is inherently good has direct detrimental effects. It is surprisingly common for abusers and, at times, victims to describe the act as "instruction" rather than abuse. Questions regarding the relative power and authority of the participants in the abuse, their individual capacity to consent, or the implications for appropriate boundaries and relationships for those involved are ignored since the myth that sex is categorically good predominates.

The historic movement in this country to provide sex education in schools recognized that sex was not being adequately addressed in homes or worship communities. Impulsive or irresponsible adolescents faced significant problems as they acted sexually with one another in ignorance of the facts. But although sex education addresses the facts about sexual behavior and may discuss legal and ethical dimensions of the behavior, the classroom often avoids discussions of morality, assuming that role will be filled by one's home or religious community.

What we know is that sex is a behavior that humans may find pleasurable and that sex (apart from in vitro fertilization) is required for the species to have progeny. In and of itself, sex is not *bad* or *good*—it is simply a normal human behavior. We also know that sex is a behavior in the context of a relationship. Therefore the *nature* of that relationship enters into our determination of how appropriate the behavior may be. Christians ascribe a spiritual component (moral code) to the conduct of sexual behavior. As a result, several complex factors enter into the judgment of whether the context for or particular act of sex is good or bad.

Myth 3: Sexual Behavior Is Strictly a Private Matter

Arguably, masturbation is the only occasion when sexual behavior is strictly private. Even then, there is often more than one person involved, at least at the level of fantasy. By its nature, sexual behavior is a communal act and therefore not entirely private. One may legitimately seek to confine sexual behavior to private settings. But to understand all sexual behavior as strictly private is to deny its communal nature and the social implications of the act.

The myth that sex is strictly a private matter may encourage isolation. The wish to preserve privacy may supersede other concerns (such as the safety of an individual). How do we feel when we hear a family arguing in public? Do we tell ourselves that the conflict is none of our affair and perhaps even feel a little embarrassed, as if we invaded the family's privacy? When sex is involved, the urge to preserve privacy may be stronger still.

The myth that sex is private is bolstered by the historically recent social construct called the "nuclear" family. To define a family as "nuclear" often denies influence by the "extended" family. It builds a social wall of privacy around the nucleus (father, mother, and children) that denies scrutiny by society, lest privacy be invaded. The notion of the privacy of the nuclear family allows the treatment of children or spouses within the nuclear family (including the sexual abuse of children or spouses) to go largely unchecked by society.

Although the privacy enjoyed by defining families as nuclear is highly regarded by many, it is not without its critics. In *Family Violence,* M. D. Pagelow writes: "Most people continue to embrace the notion that the nuclear family unit represents love, mutual protection and security, despite the fact that the media has increasingly shown the 'underside' of family life."[3] The movement away from the more traditional extended family to the more isolated nuclear family results in fewer adults available to serve as nurturing resources for children. With increased mobility and the high cost of competent child care, nuclear families are more likely to be in situations in which no one but the parents (or worse, the single parent) will share the stress of parenting and providing for a family. In 1993, Dr. S. L. Bloom wrote:

> Actually, it is time that we recognize that the nuclear family does not work, that it places an unreasonable and unhealthy burden on an already overstressed system *(that is, the family system)*, and that it is time for definitive change in the structure of our communities, housing and laws.[4]

Sex is not private, and the privacy of the nuclear family should not be held in higher regard than the safety of its members. But no wholesale invasion of family privacy is warranted either. Instead, more realistic guidelines for intruding on family privacy are preferred. When there is any credible possibility of harm to a family member, safety should be given priority over privacy. Therefore, when sexual behavior is harmful (that is, possibly abusive), it is reasonable for society to invade the privacy even of a nuclear family on behalf of the potential victim's safety. There are legal guidelines for determining when to violate family privacy. Using the law as a threshold for when privacy should be invaded would actually result in *more* reports of abuse than currently occur, since respect for privacy and fear currently cause many persons to avoid scrutinizing someone else's family.

Myth 4: Keeping Silence Protects Others

This myth is often invoked in conjunction with the prohibition against betraying one's family. The old adage "blood is thicker than water" may simply be a means to enlist others in a "conspiracy of silence" about sexual abuse and to protect the abuser. It is important to recognize that if reporting the abuse betrays the family, the abuser has *already betrayed* the victim.

To victims, keeping the secret and sacrificing themselves is often seen as a means to protect others (in or out of the family) from abuse. Abusers have even made explicit promises to victims that their secrecy ensures no one else will be abused.

The unfortunate truth is that, even if abusers wish to restrict the abuse to a single victim, typically they are not able to do so. When the abuse of other victims is discovered, the victim who kept silent in order to protect them often feels guilt. The silent victim realizes then that telling the secret would have provided more protection than his or her silence.

Unfortunately, the silent victim mistakenly takes blame for the abuse of subsequent victims, focusing on one's own silence rather than holding the offender accountable for the abuse. The coerced silence of a victim is an example of how an abuser exploits his or her power and misuses the relationship with the victim. The silence is the fault of the abuser, not the silent victim.

Myth 5: The Victim Shares Blame or Is at Fault

Experienced clinicians automatically assume that victims of sexual abuse wrongly blame themselves for the abuse. Victim self-blame is so pervasive that, not surprisingly, society often blames victims as well. Questions of seduction, consent, and compliance are often posed to the victims. Did victims voice their disapproval? Did they adequately resist sexual advances? Did they somehow invite sexual behavior by their words or how they dressed or by the circumstances under which they encountered the offenders? Eventually, these questions all lead to the fundamental belief that the victims are somehow to blame.

But the questions ignore the power, authority, and responsibility owned by the abusers. Who are the abusers and what are their patterns of sexual behavior? What influence, power, and responsibility did the offenders have at the time of the sexual abuse? What action on the abusers' part could have prevented or ended the sexual abuse? These questions, focusing on the abusers rather than the victims, often illuminate why blaming the victims is a misplaced effort.

Myth 6: Children Can Consent to Sex

Although children have been used as sexual objects throughout history, they have never been able to give undiminished consent to sexual relationships. Instead, children have historically been "possessions" that one may use as much as the laws and societal norms of the time allowed. When children were recognized as fully human with rights, the question of their consent entered more fully into the discussion. No one questions the inability of a child to consent independently to a contract or legal agreement. Why then do we suggest that children can consent to engage in sex with others?

Children cannot, in the eyes of our society, consent to engage in sexual behavior with others. Even when both participants in the sexual behavior are teenaged, most states legally recognize some age threshold necessary to imply the possible consent of the participants (below which the act constitutes statutory rape).

Consent is usually strictly defined in a legal sense, but nuances of consent are more complicated in real life. The fact that a sexual experience can be physically pleasurable to the victim can cause that victim to question to what extent he or she consented (even if the victim is legally incapable of consent). Though categorically abusive to the child victim, physical pleasure during the abuse at times presents a confusing dimension of the experience to the victim.

Myth 7: If the Victim Enjoys Sex, It's Not Abuse

Children find the complexities of relationship, physical pleasure, and the ability to consent all difficult issues. The myth that if any physical pleasure was experienced during the abuse, then the child was not really abused poses a daunting problem. This myth also maligns adults whose physical experience may have confused their perception of consent.

For many victims of sexual abuse, any pleasure they associate with the abusive experience can be emotionally distressing and confusing. Even more confusion results when the abuser is known well to the victim and occupies an important intimate role in his or her life (such as a father, spouse, or pastor). When sexual pleasure is associated with an abusive incident, victims may be unable to experience sexual pleasure in subsequent appropriate sexual relationships. This insidious result of sexual abuse plagues the future intimate relationships of many victims.

For teenaged boys in our society, pleasure may be mixed with a sense of increased social status because they "finally" had sex. Higher status coupled with the victimized boys' (ambivalent) feelings about having sex add further complications in their sexual development. These boys may become promiscuous and even sexually abusive in order to make sense of their own sexual abuse or in order to claim power and status in future sexual relationships.

Myth 8: Telling the Secret Harms the Victim

The victim of sexual abuse or one who has heard about the abuse may genuinely worry that revealing the secret will bring additional harm to the victim. Victims often believe this because the abusers have threatened outright that they will be harmed (sexually or otherwise) if they tell the secret. However, if the victim is a child, child protection laws are reasonably effective in removing the child from harm. If the victim is an adult, the risk of harm may be more credible. Although restraining orders from local police guarantee a penalty to abusers if they have any contact with their victims, offenders can do a lot of harm to the victim before they get punished. If an adult feels genuinely threatened by an abuser, domestic abuse shelters ("hidden" safe houses) grant the victim more protection than a restraining order.

Persons hearing about sexual abuse, however, may erroneously believe that if they report abuse, the abuse will increase. No case of abuse is identical to any other, but clinical experience indicates that typically the abuse stops once the offender understands his or her behavior is being monitored by someone other than the victim. As a result, keeping the secret does more harm than telling it.

Unfortunately, concern for victims' safety is invoked for wrong reasons by those who discover the abuse. Consider, for example, the following excerpt from the July 28, 2002, *Philadelphia Inquirer* report about the past response of Cardinal Anthony J. Bevilacqua of the Archdiocese of Philadelphia:

> For instance, while he disclosed on Feb. 22 that the Philadelphia Archdiocese had "credible evidence" that 35 priests, most now dead or retired, had abused about 50

minors since 1952, he has refused to disclose the priests' names to parishioners or the public, saying that could be hurtful to victims.[5]

Although it would be harmful and a further gross violation to release the names of the fifty minors, releasing the names of the charged abusers would create an environment of intolerance for sexual abuse and would suggest greater safety for past and present victims.

Myth 9: With an Adolescent, It's Not Child Abuse

Civil law can be especially confusing when determining whether sexual behavior is abusive or not. Often, rape laws vary according to the age of the victim. If a victim is younger than a certain age and is sexually active, it is considered statutory rape even if the child insists there was full consent. Again, a child is not considered capable of consent. Further, with older teens, some states require that the abuser be a certain number of years older than the victim before the act can be considered rape.

Here, the distinction between a *criminal charge*, such as rape, and a *civil* charge, such as child abuse, is important. Even if the incident does not qualify legally as *rape*, in most cases, sexual activity between a person over the age of eighteen and a minor is considered to be *child abuse* and should be reported as such. Although it is true that older adolescents are commonly drawn toward sexual activity, sex may still result in a civil charge. Sexual activity between an adult and an adolescent of any age should always be reported to the Department of Human Services.

Myth 10: Children Don't Abuse Other Children

One possible result of child sexual abuse is the original victim becoming sexually precocious (prematurely active sexually) and sexually abusing other children. Sexual abuse by children is not the developmentally common phenomenon known as "playing doctor," in which there is nonintrusive mutual exposure of genitalia by small children. The behavior considered here includes oral sexual behavior or sexual penetration or bodily violation of the victim by objects or parts of the abuser's body.

In addition to being sexually precocious children, adolescents with psychopathic personality structures may use child-to-child sexual abuse as one among many of their asocial behaviors. (Please note: Although the term "psychopathic" fell mostly into disuse for a time among mental health professionals and is not used in the diagnostic and statistical manual [DSM-IV], it has recently been reconsidered clinically. A specific set of symptoms has been developed, along with diagnostic criteria, to describe adolescents and adults who display a profound lack of conscience and engage in a broad range of asocial behaviors for the adrenaline rush they provide.) Each case of child-to-child sexual abuse needs careful professional scrutiny to determine the harm done and the cause of the behavior.

Child offenders may be prior victims, but their personal tragedy does nothing to mitigate the victimization experienced by the new victim. In these child offenders, neither the plight of the new victim, nor the possible previous abuse of the offender should be overlooked. Unfortunately, clinical experience suggests only the current victim will be adequately cared for in these instances.

For example, a ten-year-old boy was convicted of the sexual abuse of a nine-year-old neighborhood girl. He was confined for several years in a restrictive residence for conduct-disordered children and attended a group for sex-offending boys. Careful scrutiny revealed that the girl had been sexually precocious with both the ten-year-old boy and his six-year-old brother. Fearing the loss of both children, the mother of the boys "sacrificed" her older son to protect her younger son, since she believed law enforcement would recognize only males as offenders. No one ever investigated the reason for a nine-year-old girl being sexually active at such a young age, and she received no treatment.

Myth 11: Victims Imagine or Make Up Abuse Memories

The dispute regarding the possibility of repressed memories (memory of past sexual abuse forgotten for a time and newly recovered) has not been resolved in the professional community. In the 1996 publication *The Spectrum of Child Abuse: Assessment, Treatment and Prevention,* R. K. Oates cites cases in which the recovered memories of victims were later corroborated by the abuser or another family member.[6] In that same year, Daniel L. Schacter concluded in *Searching for Memory: The Brain, the Mind, and the Past:*

> We simply don't yet know whether illusory memories of sexual abuse are exceedingly rare, as some clinicians have claimed, or whether they are widespread, as critics of so-called recovered memory therapy have argued. It seems unlikely, however, that they can all be written off to just a handful of wayward therapists.[7]

If a memory emerges in the midst of therapy, the therapist has a moral and ethical responsibility to handle it in accordance with state law and in the best interest of the client. For worship communities, the problem is much simpler. If an adult discloses the recovery of a memory of child sexual abuse, the adult should be immediately referred for therapy. If a child alleges past abuse, a report must be made. It is not within the purview of the pastor or staff in a church to determine the validity of the memory.

Apart from cases of recovering a past memory, it is extremely unusual for a victim (even a child) to disclose an imagined current experience of sexual abuse or to make a false allegation intentionally. In any case, like threats of suicide, all allegations of sexual abuse should be taken seriously and reported (for children) or referred so trained professionals can help with the situation.

Myth 12: Many or Most Victims Grow Up to Be Abusers

It is true that most sex offenders were previously sexually victimized. But it takes very few abusers to produce many victims. Clinical experience suggests that only a few victims become abusers. Victims are more likely to reenact their past abuse by harming *themselves*. Most sexual abuse victims grow up sustaining the role of *perpetual victim* (at times exposing themselves to the risk of further abuse) if they do not receive therapeutic help. The greatest tragedy of this myth is that it can result in victims being singled out in the future and denied appropriate opportunities and responsibilities because of an unfounded fear that they will sexually abuse others.

Myth 13: It Only Happens Among the Poor or Minorities

When one considers the incidence of physical abuse and domestic violence, there is a positive correlation among lower socioeconomic status, the stress of unemployment, the prevalence of substance abuse, and the number of people being physically harmed.[8] For sexual abuse, however, there is no current evidence suggesting that it is any more prevalent among poor or minority people than it is among more privileged people. The motivation of sexual abusers and the factors associated with the risk for future offending (discussed later in this chapter) have nothing to do with race, ethnicity, income, or education.

This myth not only supports a prejudicial view of marginalized people, but also helps sustain the silence of victims in privileged communities. Victims in privileged communities likely already believe that if they disclose the sexual abuse, their allegations will not be taken seriously because of the social status of the abusers.

Myth 14: Offenders Are So Sick, They Should Not Be Held Responsible for Their Behavior

Andrew Vachss, a lawyer whose only clients are children, wrote an article for the July 14, 2002, *Parade* insert to the *Philadelphia Inquirer* entitled "The Difference Between 'Sick' and 'Evil.'" In it, he states: "Sickness is a condition. Evil is a behavior." Later he writes: "And just as evil is always a choice, sickness is always the absence of choice. Sickness happens. Evil is inflicted."[9]

Mr. Vachss is not the first or only person to wrestle with a distinction between sickness and evil. In *People of the Lie*, M. Scott Peck explores frightening situations that he concludes are the result of evil, rather than sick people.[10]

Alternatively, a mental health professional might suggest that sickness and evil are not mutually exclusive. Though sickness may be a condition, and though some condition or other may be diagnosed for persons who sexually abuse others, that sickness does not necessarily relieve the abusers of all responsibility for their actions. Although forensic psychological examinations may provide information about criminals' past or current states of functioning, sickness does not make their actions any less criminal. I suspect that most mental health professionals would vehemently disagree with Mr. Vachss's conclusion that a sickness always precludes choice. It is true that no one can choose to be sick or not to be sick, but only a very small group of sicknesses, in very extreme cases, deny the ill person the ability to make a choice. Even people experiencing a psychotic episode may be able to make some life choices even though his or her ability to choose in other areas of life functioning is grossly impaired.

Specific to sex offenders, the lack of consequences for their behavior is therapeutically contraindicated. Indeed, every intervention for sex offenders known to me begins with helping the offender recognize the harm done by his or her behavior, claim personal responsibility for inflicting that harm, and accepting the consequences of the inappropriate behavior (and possibly attempting to make amends for harm done). Denial of harm to the victim or denial of personal responsibility for harm done only serves to encourage sex offenders to reoffend. Among sex offenders, the myth that sickness means one cannot make choices about one's behavior nearly guarantees that the offender will harm another victim. Sex offenders are sick, *and* they are responsible for their behavior.

Myth 15: Gay Men Sexually Abuse Children

There seems to be undue confusion between the definitions of homosexuality and pedophilia (or ephebophilia, as mentioned in the previous chapter). Homosexuality refers to a pattern of sexual arousal by persons of the same (versus the opposite) sex. As such, when sexual behavior occurs between persons of the same sex, it is homosexual behavior. Pedophilia (and ephebophilia) describes the patterns of persons who act when sexually aroused by less than fully developed human bodies.

Since the pattern of sexual arousal (being sexually aroused by the underdeveloped bodies of children) is at stake for most persons who sexually abuse children, it does not seem likely that most or even many homosexual persons would sexually abuse children. But do statistics support this assertion?

In *The Culture of Fear,* B. Glassner writes: "One recent study published in the medical journal *Pediatrics* indicates that a child is about a hundred times more likely to be molested by the heterosexual partner of a close relative than by a homosexual."[11] Other research, Glassner writes, finds that many of the men who molest children not only are not gay, but also despise gay people.

Just as heterosexual adults are not usually sexually aroused by the underdeveloped bodies of opposite sex children, it is unreasonable to believe homosexual adults would be sexually aroused by the underdeveloped bodies of same-sex children.

Regardless of the theological or moral stance one takes regarding homosexual behavior, fearing that someone will sexually abuse children just because one is gay is not statistically or scientifically justifiable. This myth not only unjustly singles out gay persons, but also diverts attention from the statistically larger number of nonhomosexual child sex abusers and could invite prevention efforts that ignore those abusers.

Myth 16: If Married, They Would Not Abuse

Irrespective of one's view of mandatory celibacy among some clergy, there is no evidence to support that married persons sexually abuse others less than unmarried persons. Married men have more immediate access to victims (their own children) than do unmarried men, and father-daughter incest constitutes as high of a number of child sexual abuse cases.

As with theological discussions regarding homosexuality, theological discussions regarding celibate clergy are separate from the problem of sexual abuse.

Myth 17: Older Adults Don't Sexually Abuse Children

It is true that, statistically, older sex-offending adults demonstrate less risk of repeating the sexual abuse (see the discussion of risk factors later in this chapter); but advanced age constitutes only a small reduction in the risk of repeat offending and certainly does not eliminate the possibility of future sexual abuse.

Older adults, such as grandfathers or great-uncles, who have easy access to children, are identified in some substantiated cases of child sexual abuse. Just as sexuality among older adults can no longer be ignored, likewise the potential for sexual abuse by older adults should not be summarily discounted. Subscribing to this myth may result in either a false sense of safety because a caregiver is elderly or in refusing to believe the allegation of abuse because the alleged abuser is old.

Myth 18: Child Pornography Isn't Sexual Abuse

As previously mentioned, sexualized or pornographic images of children are readily available on-line. But is this truly child sexual abuse? The child whose image is reproduced or whose face is integrated into a computer-generated image is never a consenting participant in the process. It not only is psychologically damaging to the child, but also constitutes a violation of the law to produce or transmit child pornographic images.

Further, if one's sexual desire is stimulated by underdeveloped human bodies, access to child pornographic images may serve as "triggers" for abusive behavior by the sex offender, as described in the next section of this chapter.

Myth 19: These Are All of the Myths That Exist

Of course this list is not exhaustive. Not everyone subscribes to these myths, nor does anyone likely subscribe to all of them all of the time. But since our actions, responses, and reactions are tempered by our attitudes and beliefs, we would do well to think about when, or at what level, we may discover ourselves to be motivated by these myths. Though *consciously* disagreeing with these myths, one may find his or her actions *unconsciously* motivated by them. Especially when myths are part of our socialized belief system from an early age (such as sex is bad), they can have an unconscious effect on our responses.

ABUSERS: WHAT WE THINK—
AND SOME THINGS WE KNOW

In his 1995 dissertation, "Prevention and the Roman Catholic Clergy," Dr. Robert Thornton reviewed several current theories for understanding what he calls "the dynamics and categorization of sexually exploitive helping profession- als," that is, why do some religious leaders engage in sexual abuse?[12]

One theory suggests four types of abusers:

- Those who are psychotic (out of touch with reality)
- Predatory psychopaths (persons without any con- science planning abuse)
- Persons with severe narcissistic or borderline person- ality disorders
- Passive, self-destructive helpers who are controlled or intimidated by those they seek to help[13]

One may readily note how the fourth category unfortunately shifts blame for the abuse to the victim.

A second theory identifies three patterned categories for abuse:

- A pattern of abuse ("professional incest") similar to parent-child incest in its emphasis of age differences, misuse of intrinsic trust, unequal power and authority, intellectual differences, and psychological vulnerability
- A pattern of abuse similar to rape in its use of power, physical force, intimidation, or coercion
- A pattern of opportunistic exploitation of the disa- bility (intellectual or psychological) of the intended victim[14]

A third theory uses a model of addiction to understand the sex offenders' motivation. Their sexual addiction is defined as repetitive, uncontrolled sexual activity of any kind. Sexual addicts typically have in common: being previously and severely abused themselves, feeling shameful and unworthy, codependency, and using sexual activity to take care of their emotional needs, among others.[15]

These theories use clinical experience to try to understand the motivation behind a behavior that (thankfully) simply cannot be understood by most people.

My experience doing risk assessments with sex offenders has prompted a different approach for understanding what motivates sex abusers. Instead of beginning with a theory to understand the behavior, I examine the factors that are most predictive of future reoffending.

Over the years, structured assessments have been developed to measure the risk of reoffending known sex offenders. It is, perhaps, not too presumptuous to conclude that whatever prompts them to offend again (even after being caught once) was likely an important motivation for them to offend in the first place. A more complete description of risk for recidivism and of assessment tools, though interesting, is not required for purposes of this discussion.[16] However, as a result of my work doing assessments of sex offenders, the following motivations for people engaging in sex-offending behavior are suggested:

1. INTRUSIVE SEXUAL THOUGHTS/OBSESSIVE RUMINATION ON SEX

Persons in this category have specific types of people (including young, old, male, female, those with certain physical features, those of a particular race or ethnicity, and so on), or things (such as clothing, images, animals, and so on) that they find sexually arousing. These persons or things are often called the abuser's "triggers." Any exposure to one's specific triggers may be followed by sexual thoughts. An abuser may think obsessively about the triggers, and the sexual thoughts may so frequently intrude on everyday thinking that the person feels powerless to stop, no matter what else the person is doing. Often persons in this category have been sexually victimized themselves.

For abusers in this category, the behavior is all about sexual stimulation and sexual gratification. These people may fall into one of two subtypes:

a. impulsive
b. predatory

The *impulsive* person, with intrusive or obsessive sexual thoughts, acts on an opportunity for sexual gratification without thought for the consequences (to himself or herself or to the victim). These people often have marked negative emotional reactions to their own impulsive behavior and may become suicidal after this "unplanned" behavior because they feel so much shame.

The *predatory* person, with intrusive or obsessive sexual thoughts, feels so consumed by one's thoughts that he or she plans a way to manipulate, coerce, or seduce the victim into giving the sexual gratification sought. Predatory persons' behavior is planned, perhaps even calculated, but they also feel driven to the behavior.

People of both subtypes may feel as though their offending behavior is an addiction they cannot end or a compulsion that they cannot stop themselves from doing. In reality, there are often measures these persons can take prior to acting sexually that can interrupt their "cycle of abuse" (such as turning away from a trigger, intentionally interrupting obsessive thoughts, avoiding high-risk situations, stopping when beginning to act) and prevent themselves from sexually abusing others. Even an obsessive person need not be compelled to act.

2. OFFENDING AS AN EXPRESSION OF CONTROL OR VIOLENCE

Persons in this category can likewise act impulsively or in a planned fashion, but their purpose has almost nothing to do with sexual gratification. These persons may be like the one's described above, "narcissistic" or "borderline" or "incestuous." At the heart of their behavior is not a wish for sexual gratification, but rather a wish to use sexual behavior as an expression of authority, dominance, or violence. These offenders may engage in pedophilic or ephebophilic sex or may engage in rape. These persons may experience guilt or shame about other things, but they often feel justified, or even helpful, in their sexual behavior toward their victims. Clinical experience suggests that these persons have personal histories that likely include physical, rather than sexual, abuse in which they were likewise controlled by others.

3. PSYCHOPATHY AND SEX OFFENDING

There is an emerging, clearer definition for the clinical term "psychopathy." To be diagnosed as a psychopath, one must demonstrate a series of personal characteristics to a professional assessor. These characteristics or symptoms fall within two dimensions: emotional/interpersonal and social deviance. The first dimension describes a psychopath as glib and superficial, egocentric and grandiose, lacking remorse or guilt, lacking empathy, deceitful and manipulative, and having shallow emotions. The second dimension describes psychopaths as impulsive, having poor behavioral controls, needing excitement, lacking responsibility, and demonstrating early behavior problems as well as adult anti-social behaviors.[17]

Some professionals suggest that all sex abusers are psychopaths. In *Psychopathy: Antisocial, Criminal, and Violent Behavior,* contributor Darwin Dorr writes: "Asserted more boldly, it is argued that pedophilia may represent a special case, or subcase of psychopathy."[18] In the same book, however, Robert Hare notes a higher rate of psychopathy only among sex offenders but not among the general population (26.1 percent to 30.5 percent of child molesters in two different studies).[19] There is no clinical evidence to support the claim that *all* sex offenders, or even all pedophiles, are psychopathic as Dorr asserts. There appears to be debilitating shame and guilt among a subset of sex offenders. Beyond studies concerning pedophiles exclusively, cases of psychopathy in sex offenders, even among repeat or serial rapists, are estimated at only half of those convicted.[20]

A significant problem with the assertion that all pedophiles or all sex abusers are psychopaths is the poor prognosis for the successful treatment of psychopaths. In prison, designation as psychopathic could mean that an inmate's requests for parole are automatically denied. That inmate may also be excluded from rehabilitative programs since there is little chance such costly programs would be effective. For sex abusers, designation as a psychopath could mean abject, unforgiving rejection with no efforts at rehabilitation: "If you are dealing with a true psychopath it is important to recognize that the current prognosis for improvement in his or her behavior is poor. . . . The best strategy is to avoid becoming entangled with a psychopath in the first place."[21] It is important to recognize whether sexual abuse is one among a repertoire of asocial behaviors indulged in by a psychopath. It is equally important to recognize that not all sex abusers are psychopaths. Efforts at treatment for these two groups would vary significantly.

The use of risk measures and work with sex offenders establishes that some interventions, though not eliminating the risk of reoffending, do in fact significantly reduce the risk of reoffending in those who are not psychopaths.

3

Some Solutions: Prevention and Response

*In the morning sow your seed, and at evening do not
let your hands be idle; for you do not know which will
prosper, this or that, or whether both alike will be
good. (Ecclesiastes 11:6)*

CONTAINING AND MANAGING RISK

I f things stay as they have been, spending a year in the
United States of America can be risky business. Out of
every 100,000 people in the U.S., 4,124 will be documented victims of murder, rape, robbery, or aggravated
assault; nearly 3,618 will be documented victims of burglary,
larceny, auto theft, or property crime; 200 will die of cancer;
266 will die from problems related to heart disease; 16 will
die of Alzheimer's disease; 15 will die in motor vehicle acci-
dents; 10 will commit suicide; 60 will die from stroke; 133
will suffer from gonorrhea; 254 will suffer from chlamydia;
and 13 will suffer from syphilis. Out of every 1,000 live
births, 48 will be to teenaged mothers; and nearly 7 other
"birthing" infants will die. Eighty people in the entire United
States will die in tornadoes, and 89 people here will die from
being struck by lightning.[1]

Living here or anywhere includes risk. But God did not create humans as passive recipients of the circumstances life deals them. Being a victim is *not* the same as being a passive recipient. Life can be risky even for persons who may not be "easy targets."

As active participants in our lives and our world, people and organizations can make choices that limit the likelihood of bad things happening if we know how to do so. Risk can be "contained," or "managed," if one makes a conscious effort to do so. Often, risk cannot be entirely eliminated.

Congregations can make conscious efforts to reduce the risk of sexual (and physical) abuse in their congregations, even if they cannot categorically prohibit it.

"Risk containment" is my description of efforts aimed at reducing or containing the risk that abusers will readily gain access to the worshiping community. "Risk management" is a description of efforts that recognize the possible presence of abusers in the congregation and are aimed at managing that risk, that is, at reducing the opportunity or circumstances that would allow them to be abusive.

In downtown Philadelphia, there are terrific movie theaters that feature provocative and interesting foreign and art films. There is one such theater in a far northern suburb of the city. Going to the downtown theaters involves an increased risk for becoming a victim of urban crime (robbery, auto theft, assault, and so on). One can contain the risk by avoiding the downtown theaters and traveling a substantial distance to the north suburb. Even though one does not eliminate the possibility of victimization, the risk is greatly reduced. Risk reduction by risk containment does not come without a price, however. More money is spent on gas, ticket prices may be higher, traveling time to and from the theater may be longer, and a single theater offers far less selection than do several multiscreen theaters concentrated downtown.

Should one decide that the cost of containing risk is not worth the benefit of reducing the risk? Or should one recognize that risk still remains no matter which theater is attended, and efforts at risk management (to "manage" the risk that exists) may be engaged? One could park only in an attended parking lot; travel in a group; walk only in well-lit, populated places; or visit the theaters during traditionally low-crime hours of the day.

In any case, even if all measures for risk containment and management are utilized, there is no guarantee that bad things are categorically precluded. Although there are some risks that can be completely eliminated (for example, the risk of pregnancy can be prevented by keeping sperm from coming in contact with an egg), most risk can be only contained or managed.

Every congregation is obviously different from another, despite some similarities. And although general suggestions for abuse *prevention* (efforts to contain and manage risk) can be made, the specific application of suggestions to particular congregations requires a clear understanding of any unique circumstances in those congregations. Further, and perhaps more important, suggestions for prevention are best viewed as "categories," or samples of prevention strategies, rather than as a conclusive list. If each congregation collectively considers how the risk of abuse can be avoided (risk containment) and how any existing risk can be limited or reduced (risk management), the congregation may add pragmatic prevention measures not included in the following guidelines and perhaps even unique to their particular circumstance.

A PRACTICAL APPROACH TO PREVENTION

Churches are often very busy places with limited human resources. Honest pastors will be the first to admit that they do not work a forty-hour week. One governing body defined a full-time work week for pastors as fifty-five or more hours a week. Therefore, compelling motivation is needed for a church to spend the time required in developing a plan to prevent sexual abuse. Four such motivating factors are: the need to create sanctuary, the desire to limit exposure to legal action, the need to prevent false allegations, and the desire to prevent abuse.

1. Creating Sanctuary

But you, O LORD, are a shield around me. (Ps. 3:3)
O LORD, my God, in you I take refuge. (Ps. 7:1)
The LORD is a stronghold for the oppressed. (Ps. 9:9)
In the LORD I take refuge. (Ps. 11:1)
You, O LORD, will protect us; you will guard us from this generation forever. (Ps. 12:7)
Protect me, O God, for in you I take refuge. (Ps. 16:1)

Many people consider the word "sanctuary" to refer to an architectural structure, but it also means a refuge, or place of safety. Historically, worship communities as well as their buildings have provided sanctuary to others. When sexual abuse is associated with worship community workers, a historic moral mandate is violated along with the law. The spiritual implications of this double violation will be discussed in the next chapter. But any discussion of prevention measures should be informed by our recognition of this double violation. An implicit covenant with congregation members is broken when members are abused (especially when they are abused by staff) in the very organization that was supposed to be a place of sanctuary.[2] If sanctuary is truly a part of the identity of a worship community, and not just a pleasant idea or an abstract concept, prevention is not optional. Prevention becomes another way in which the worship community "lives out" its moral commitment. This rationale may seem obvious, but at every one of my presentations to churches or synagogues, my suspicion that financial and legal concerns alone motivate the effort has been voiced by someone in attendance.

Establishing the creation of sanctuary as a primary motivation for prevention denies the cynical view that prevention measures are instituted merely in an effort to cover the "corporate behinds" of congregations. Because there is a corporate component to every organization, some people fear that worship communities could be viewed as "just another business." The mandate for creating sanctuary is recognition that worship communities are distinct from businesses and have additional motivation for prevention efforts that are far removed from sustaining a positive corporate bottom line.

2. Providing Legal Protection

Having established the creation of a genuine sanctuary as a primary motivation, it is notable that there are also legal benefits (with attendant financial benefits) to practicing prevention. An allegation of sexual abuse can easily result in a lawsuit against the alleged offender, the worship community, and the associated denomination. Large settlements, in and out of court, have been paid to victims by congregations and denominations for which the offenders worked. Members of various congregations have expressed outrage that contributions made for the ministry of their congregations or denominations may instead have been used to compensate a victim of abuse or as "hush money" to keep the allegation out of the courts.[3] These congregants seldom begrudge reparations to victims for the victims' sakes but resent the use of their contributions for purposes other than those originally intended.

The court is responsible not only to judge guilt and innocence, but also to judge who is culpable for the harm done and to what extent those found culpable share responsibility for making reparations. If the denomination or congregation has made an effort in good faith to prevent the possibility of abuse and to respond appropriately should abuse occur, the court will be more likely to judge that congregation less culpable if the alleged offender is found guilty. Likewise, the congregation or denomination will likely share less legal (and financial) responsibility for making reparations to the victim. In addition, morally and psychologically, the worship community's role of ministry and healing toward the victim is greatly enhanced if the community is judged not to have enabled the offender.

3. Limiting False Allegations

It is remarkable that most conversations between me and administrators from various denominations about abuse in churches and synagogues lead to a discussion of false allegations. There seems to be an almost immediate fear on the part of administrators that any discussion of or actions for sexual abuse education or prevention may actually invite false allegations. The administrators' fears are typically couched in the belief that any discussion of or action by a congregation is tantamount to the admission of an existing problem. In reality, sexual abuse prevention is the admission of an existing risk!

If reasonable prevention measures are instituted and sustained, the congregation will be more conscious of situations that may allow sexual abuse and will limit those situations and circumstances that provide opportunities for offenders to abuse. Conscious efforts for prevention likewise limit compromising situations that an unscrupulous person could otherwise exploit to make a false allegation. False allegations are also more credibly denied when prevention measures are part of the normal fabric of worship community activities. Abuse prevention becomes a tool, therefore, not only to protect victims, but also to provide protection to valuable staff that may otherwise be more vulnerable to false allegations.

4. Limiting the Occurrence of Abuse

Ultimately, of course, the purpose of prevention measures is to protect potential victims. One wishes that this reason alone would motivate prevention efforts in worship communities. The sad fact is that continual and repeated victimization did not command the attention of our nation until large legal settlements were associated with the incidence of abuse. What else could explain the silent "see no evil" posture of the Roman Catholic Church and of society in general following the initial publication of *A Gospel of Shame*? A recent book entitled *Betrayal,* written by "the investigative staff of *The Boston Globe,*"[4] notes that their first article about clergy abuse in America's "quintessential Catholic city" was published in January 2002, but their work was preceded by the work of Jason Berry in other newspapers (including the *National Catholic Reporter*) since 1985 and Berry's 1992 exposé entitled *Lead Us Not into Temptation: Catholic Priests and the Sexual Abuse of Children.*[5]

What can explain the continuing denial of non-Catholic congregations even after the crisis has come to light in the Roman Catholic Church? How many more lawsuits in other denominations will it take before we admit we all share in the risk of sexual abuse being discovered within our own worship community? Should money be the only true motivation for action by communities of faith? Both adults and children have been victimized and continue to be victimized. Limiting the occurrence of sexual abuse, along with preserving identity as a sanctuary, constitutes ample motivation to institute prevention without delay. The U.S. Advisory Board on Child Abuse and Neglect declared the problem a national emergency in their 1990 publication and specifically asked "religious institutions" to join as part of the solution in their 1991 publication, writing:

> The Board believes that, because of their broad base and deep historic roots, as well as their accessibility to children, family, neighborhood, and community, religious institutions often possess a unique capacity to initiate those activities necessary for the promotion of a responsive community child

protection system. Moreover, where necessary, they are often able to foster the accountability of that system.

Responsibility for solving the complex problem of child maltreatment cannot be placed at the doorstep of the nation's religious institutions. Still, the Board believes that—because they have been, and will continue to be, an integral part of neighborhood and community life—their potential as agents of positive change in connection with child maltreatment needs to be tapped more effectively.[6]

RISK CONTAINMENT

With regard to worship communities and their associated denomination organizations, the risk of abuse is contained when offenders have less access to positions of power or influence.[7] There are two readily accessible strategies for limiting this access: (1) the use of psychological assessments with ministry candidates and (2) the use of background checks by applicants for *all* positions in the worship community.

1. The Use and Limits of Psychological Assessments

Many religious organizations mandate psychological assessments for candidates seeking leadership positions. Though apparently expensive, these assessments are not so costly when one considers their benefits and interprets the cost as distributed across all the years of service the candidate will provide. If your congregation or denomination does not require these evaluations, the following discussion is provided to support an effort to persuade them to do so.

Psychological tests have been developed to provide valid and reliable indications of a variety of aspects of personality functioning. Some psychological tests are structured groups of questions that a person answers about oneself. Other tests are activities or tasks the person completes without knowing what is being measured and which reveal aspects of how that person functions in the world. These tests can be compared to determine how a candidate "wishes to be seen" and how he or she appears to be actually functioning at that time. Good tests are standardized in terms of how they are administered and scored and normed, based upon most peoples' functioning. A normed and standardized test provides a more consistent measure for all candidates and can help remove biases in interpretation based upon age, sex, race, education, and so on. No single test, however, can provide a reliable picture of how the person functions on the whole.

Some people (and some courts) confuse psychologists with psychiatrists. Psychological assessments are different from psychiatric assessments. Psychiatrists use their vast clinical experience and their training as physicians to investigate a patient's reported symptoms in order to diagnose and treat mental illnesses.

Psychological assessments use several psychological tests, extensive personal and family history, clinical interviews, and clinical observation to inform the psychologist's work.[8] Since some tests are easier to "fake" than others, the use of a variety of tests makes faking less likely and typically reveals it when it does happen. The psychologist integrates all the information. The assessor uses clinical experience, psychological education, and training to develop a more complete picture of the person's *current* functioning. A state that grants a license to a psychologist indicates to the consumer that the professional has met specific education and training requirements and should be competent to do psychological work. Although several professions provide training to conduct therapy, only psychologists may conduct psychological assessments (just as physicians are typically the only ones allowed to prescribe medications).

Since no picture of personality functioning is ever exhaustive, there are aspects about the person that may not be conclusively known. On the other hand, assessments do reliably highlight strengths and identify weaknesses. The assessor may suggest remediation for identified weaknesses that can affect how the person behaves in and with the congregation.

Persons being assessed often gain insights about themselves and their interactions with others, which they can use to improve personal performance and to better understand and empathize with others.

A complete psychological assessment should include an exploration of the person's psychosexual development and the integration of sexuality into personal identity. The resulting personality profile could give substantial clues as to whether the person is a sex offender. Psychological assessments cannot, however, predict the choices a person will make regarding specific future behaviors (such as sex offending). Psychological assessments are not foolproof and are only as accurate as the data used to complete them. Trained, licensed professionals are responsible for both ensuring the accuracy of assessments and noting their limitations. Although psychological assessments may do much successfully to limit access to worship communities by some offenders, that is neither their greatest strength nor their primary purpose. Assessments are excellent tools for religious organizations to use with leadership candidates to identify potential problems, suggest remediation for weaknesses, and make the most of the person's strengths.

2. The Use of Background Checks

Nothing is more effective in predicting future behavior than a person's past practice.[9] As a result, in general, persons who have offended in the past present a known risk of offending again and should not be allowed access to potential victims.

Often persons with access to children in academic and health care facilities are routinely expected to provide proof of a history of appropriate behavior in the form of background checks. Incomprehensibly, this practice has been adopted by woefully few worship communities.

Background checks vary little from state to state and typically take two forms. The first is a check for any record of criminal behavior and is usually provided through the state police. The second is a check for any unresolved or sustained charge of child abuse and is usually available through the state's Department of Human Services.[10] For a nominal fee, usually paid by the person seeking the position, the background checks are conducted in the person's most recent state of residence, and an affidavit confirming no offenses is sent to the designated organization (in this case, the local congregation).

For worship communities, volunteers often make up a substantial portion of their workforce. In large congregations that can afford to do so, requiring background checks of volunteers is highly recommended. If it is not reasonable to obtain checks on volunteers, some process of screening volunteers would be appropriate. In small communities, one may speak to persons who know the volunteer well, and in any case, volunteers who work with children can be asked to sign a statement indicating there are no open allegations or substantiated charges in their past. All paid staff should be required to provide current background checks at the time of employment.

Instituting a policy of conducting background checks can be met with distaste in worship communities since some people may construe such a policy to imply a lack of trust of the particular individuals currently serving the church. Therefore, *how* the new policy is introduced becomes as important as the need to introduce the policy in the first place. My past experience suggests that simply appealing to the "good business sense" of those who find the new policy distasteful is not very effective. Often their defensive reply is to note the distinction between a worship community and a secular business. One may be more successful by appealing to the compassion of the current staff who would be required to obtain the new background checks. Noting that if one institutes the policy now when staff positions are filled by trustworthy persons, then in the future, the policy will be an ordinary part of the routine and no one will look askance.

Doing it now when everyone is above reproach ensures the safety of those we seek to protect well into the future without insult to anyone.

RISK MANAGEMENT

Since nothing will categorically preclude the presence of sex offenders in a worship community, several prevention measures can be used to lower the risk that they could successfully abuse a victim. These measures need not be rigid or harsh to be effective, but they must be clearly defined and consistently followed. Although large congregations may need to impose prevention measures in a structured, formal fashion, most of these measures can be applied with equal efficacy, but less formally, in small congregations.

1. Physical Considerations

The "physical plant," or buildings, used by each congregation varies greatly. Nevertheless, some prevention measures can be applied in most settings. The following is far from an exhaustive list of solutions, but these *categories* for prevention can be used by thoughtful administrators in the congregation to generate solutions pertinent to their particular space.

Freedom of Movement—To what extent is there an opportunity for unmonitored access to buildings? Most urban congregations are forced to attend to issues of access, but many suburban or rural congregations do not. Since many people may have keys to locked exterior doors, congregations may consider local alarms on all but a minimum of local doors. These inexpensive devices are available at most hardware stores and may likewise be used on certain interior doors to limit access to physically remote areas of large buildings.

Hidden Activity—To what extent can others hide their activities while in the congregation's buildings? Although it is important to limit the number of unmonitored comings and goings at congregation buildings, it is equally important to limit privacy in these public places. It is important to note that a conversation can be private and confidential without the room being categorically private. Doors to rooms used for confidential conversations can be closed but should not be locked. Ideally, interior doors could include windows that reduce the interference of noise without blocking the view of room activities from outside the room.

Certainly, particular aspects of your local congregation's buildings may make some suggested solution untenable for your location. Nevertheless, a reasoned examination of how unmonitored movement can be limited and hidden activity avoided in your physical plant could yield changes that contribute significantly to prevention without inhibiting community activities.

2. Practices That Limit False Allegations

To decrease false allegations, increase the scrutiny by staff and congregation members of the behavior of staff and volunteers. When seen as a means to protect staff, this scrutiny can be perceived by staff as something positive rather than untrusting or even punitive. Again in this case, *how* prevention measures are introduced (for the benefit of staff rather than because of mistrust) is almost as important as introducing them. Since most abuse seems to be directed toward children, these practices likewise emphasize safety for children.

Two Adult Rule—Activities in a heavily trafficked area with frequent and easy outside observation may not require two adults to be present, but many activities do not meet those specifications. Having two adults present not only maintains accountability (check and balance), but also can be a source of responsible help in case of injury or emergency. Very small congregations may substitute close proximity to other adults in the building if two adults cannot always be present.

Open Door Policy—If interior doors have no windows, they should never be locked. Unless noise or some other problem makes it unfeasible, doors should be left open during activities. For very small children who might wander out open doors, portable gates can block their exit without closing the door.

Transportation of Children—Express written permission of parents or guardians should be obtained any time children are transported for worship community activities. The permission should acknowledge by name those people who will be providing the transportation. In this way, no one has unexpected access to children under the guise of providing transportation.

Release of Young Children—Young children should be allowed to leave an activity only when accompanied by a parent or guardian or a parent-designated responsible caregiver (such as an older sibling).

Supervision of Activities—Church or synagogue staff can provide periodic, unexpected observation of activities in an unobtrusive way, limiting the illusion that unmonitored activities are allowed in the community. The observer should be aware of the interactions of children with one another since children can be offenders as well as victims.

Monitoring Appropriate Touch—Despite fears to the contrary, reasonable measures for abuse prevention do not limit the care and nurture we provide to one another or to children. Hugging is not prohibited; in fact, it is encouraged with very young children as long as it is appropriate. Touching one another can be interpreted in three ways *by the person being touched*.[11] "Good touch" makes that person feel affirmed, cared for, supported, and good about himself or herself. "Bad touch" makes that person feel harmed, violated, disregarded, or in pain or danger. "Confusing touch" makes him or her feel uncomfortable, conflicted, or confused. As members of the community touch one another, monitoring the reaction (verbal and nonverbal cues) of those touched will limit confusing or bad touch. It is always a good idea simply to ask, "May I give you hug?" before doing so.

Monitoring the Dynamics of Relationships—Those who care for or counsel others occupy an important position of trust. Sex abuse can be the eventual result of weakening interpersonal boundaries. What does that mean? It means that the boundaries of the relationship should continually be scrutinized by the caregiver or counselor. It would be ideal if the person who is cared for or counseled could be in charge of setting limits to the relationship. However, at times of distress, that person may not be able or willing to set those boundaries appropriately, and it becomes the responsibility of those working with that person.

Counselors and caregivers can ask themselves a series of questions to help monitor their relationships.[12] Do any of their behaviors or conversations with the persons need to be kept secret (as opposed to keeping appropriate confidentiality regarding what they tell you)? A good test for secrecy is whether the caregivers or counselors would be comfortable discussing their relationship to the congregants confidentially with peers. Do they find themselves paying special attention to the attire and appearance of the persons they care for? Are gifts given or received? What is the meaning of the giving of gifts? Are the gifts appropriate? Do the counselors or caregivers feel discomfort, dread, or a rush of excitement when with the persons they are caring for? These and similar questions, honestly asked and answered, help the "helpers" do good instead of harm and avoid violating appropriate boundaries.

All of the practices listed above can be applied in worship communities of any size without great financial expense and without disrupting the character or quality of community activities. They are designed to provide safety without causing everyone to become hypervigilant. When they become an ordinary part of a worship community's daily life, they quietly prevent abuse and limit false allegations without being intrusive and without limiting natural, appropriate nurture among congregation members.

3. The Need for and Elements of a Prevention Policy

There are at least three reasons why a policy for abuse prevention should be put in writing. First, when the policy is articulated, it is clearer and better understood than if it is inferred. Writing down an articulated policy allows everyone "to get on the same page" with regard to what is expected. Second, if a policy is written, it documents a good-faith effort on the part of the community to prevent abuse, which can be vital should there ever be legal action against it. Third, a written policy for prevention really isn't that difficult to write, costs nothing, and offers a sense of sanctuary to members of the worship community.

Worries about what a policy should include and how comprehensive its scope should be generally exaggerate the importance of the document. One would do well to keep in mind that some written policy is better than no written policy; that the policy sets a tone for the worship community rather than regulating it; that the policy is not a legal document requiring finely tuned language; and the policy is less important than the actual practice in the worship community.

The elements of a prevention policy, in most cases, have already been discussed in this chapter. They include:

- A theological basis for the policy
- A statement of intent for the policy (noting both prevention of sexual abuse and prevention of false allegations)
- Guidelines for background checks and volunteer screening
- Considerations for the physical plant
- Practice guidelines for activities

SEXUAL MISCONDUCT POLICY

Obviously, one hopes that if the foregoing elements of the prevention policy are consistently practiced, there will be no need for a sexual misconduct policy. But even the soundest policy and most "religious" observance of the policy does not guarantee that no allegation will ever be made. Further, the worship community needs to know how to respond when an allegation of abuse (physical or sexual) is made by a child. Even if the victim does not accuse church staff (for example, a person alleges that a family member or family friend abused him or her), the worship community may be the sanctuary where the victim seeks assistance, and the church should be ready to respond appropriately.

The laws of each state vary as to the legal requirement to report an allegation of abuse. Some states, such as Pennsylvania, require anyone who functions in a professional capacity with a child and has sufficient reason to suspect, or is told by the child, that the child has been abused must report it to the Department of Human Services. In New Jersey, any person, even if not a professional, having a reasonable suspicion or information of alleged abuse from a child must report it. For worship communities, one hopes the community will not worry about whether they are legally mandated reporters. Instead, appealing to moral conscience and trusting in the specialized training of professional investigators, one hopes an allegation or reasonable suspicion of sexual (or physical) abuse would always and immediately be reported. It is worth noting, however, that if a mandated reporter fails to report, some state penalties may include a fine, conviction of a misdemeanor, and imprisonment.[13]

Whether an allegation is against a staff member, a volunteer, someone else, or even oneself, reporting the allegation usually works in everyone's favor. If the allegation is true, the victim is protected. When reported, professionals trained in abuse investigations interview the victim without "contaminating" their testimony (by not asking leading or "suggesting" questions). If the offender reports himself or herself for a true allegation, his or her demonstrated compliance with getting help typically reduces the severity of the potential punishment.

If the allegation is false, trained investigators are better equipped to uncover the lie and the motivation for the lie, and the alleged offender demonstrates lack of guilt by cooperating with the process. Further, repeated false allegations by the same person are recorded and grant the accuser less power to harm others with the lie since the pattern of behavior has been documented. Attempts by members of the worship community to investigate the allegation or delay or avoid reporting the allegation can contaminate the subsequent investigation or can constitute a cover-up (obstruction of justice). As a result, the sexual misconduct policy provides not *suggestions* for handling abuse allegations, but *rules* that must be followed.

The rules for reporting should be simple and clear. They pertain to children—meaning anyone younger than eighteen years old. If there is an allegation from a child or reasonable suspicion of abuse, a report should be made the same day or first thing the next day. Some organizations designate one person to be responsible for making the telephone call to report allegations. However, the person to whom the child discloses is responsible to report the allegation if the designated person fails to do so. Reports are kept anonymous and the caller does not have to have all the details before reporting an allegation. It is the job of the investigators to get the information and ascertain whether the abuse has occurred.

A detailed interview with the child or the alleged offender is not necessary. A telephone number (hotline) is typically available from each state Department of Human Services for reporting and should be readily available to staff. Persons who make a report for the first time typically feel upset and a little intimidated by the whole process. Almost invariably, however, they describe great relief after making the telephone call since the trained person who takes the report has dealt with all sorts of people and that professional helps them through the process. After the telephone conversation, a written report is also typically made. Again, the person making the report need not be fearful of not having all the information or even all the correct information. The investigative staff typically helps the reporter fill in as much as he or she knows, understanding that the reporter can only be the source of a limited amount of information.

A very brave and compassionate approach to handling allegations would be for the person suspecting abuse to contact the alleged offender (if one knows the alleged offender has a relationship with that person, and it is safe for one to do so). The alleged offender is informed of the allegation and encouraged to report the allegation at that moment. One could provide the alleged offender with the appropriate telephone number and offer to stay with him or her through the reporting process. The alleged offender should be assured that if he or she is unable to report the allegation immediately, you will do so for that person. If the alleged abuse includes any physical violence, this approach may not be safe and should be avoided. But if the allegation is of sexual abuse of a child, this approach can send a firm but compassionate message to both the alleged offender (continued support since innocent until proved guilty) and to the victim ("We hear you and are taking your concern seriously").

It should be noted that the response of most sex offenders is fairly predictable when a report is made.[14] The offender typically denies all allegations outright and will often vilify the child who disclosed (for example, calling her a pathological liar). The offender may admit the offense and promise to get help if no report is made. Offenders are rarely known for adequately addressing their problem without being forced to do so (Often facing their problem means they also face the aspects of their own past victimization they have avoided for years). It is not unlikely that frightened victims will change their story, especially if they feel intimidated by the abuser.

The need to report remains even if the child tells you it was a lie. It is the professional investigator's job to decide the veracity of the initial charge. Finally, a nonoffending parent may adamantly deny the allegation. Alternatively, a parent who is not accused of abuse may need help to escape a dangerous situation if the offender is physically violent.

It is likely that if a child is judged to be in potential danger because the alleged offender lives in the victim's home, either the child will be *temporarily* removed, or, more likely, the alleged offender will be asked to leave until the investigation is complete. After the investigation, the allegation is substantiated, unsubstantiated, or inconclusive.[15] If unsubstantiated, nothing more happens. If substantiated or inconclusive, help is provided to the victim. The alleged offender may be punished and may receive treatment. Often, family intervention is also provided. Not every offender is punished and sent to jail, as many family members fear.

Apart from allegations of child sexual abuse, the sexual misconduct policy will also likely apply to allegations of rape, nonconsensual sexual conduct toward an adult, sexual malfeasance toward an adult (sexual conduct within a ministerial or professional relationship), and sexual harassment of an adult. The policy would include rules for reporting (within the church or denomination and, when appropriate, to legal authorities and insurance carriers) and some discussion about ecclesiastical as well as judicial responses to the allegation.

Well-written policies also include a plan to provide pastoral care to alleged victims and to alleged perpetrators and to their families. An often overlooked dimension of the problem is the damage done to the congregation as a whole when sexual misconduct occurs in the church. Again, well-written policies encourage formal and pastoral discussions with the members of the congregation not immediately involved, since silence may appear to condone or cover up the violation. Finally, the policy should institute a training program for all staff and volunteers.[16]

4

Understanding Victims

How long must I bear pain in my soul,
and have sorrow in my heart all day long?
How long shall my enemy be exalted over me?
(Psalm 13:2)

lthough it may seem quite difficult, it is imperative for pastors to understand the victims of sexual abuse if pastoral care is to be done effectively. The difficulty in understanding victims of sexual abuse stems from the chaotic nature often observed in the thoughts, behaviors, and relationships of victims of sexual abuse. Sexual abuse is one kind of severe trauma that affects its victims in varying ways both immediately and over the long term. Though almost anyone would express compassion toward a victim of sexual abuse, living with the victim for a long time can be challenging. Spouses, loved ones, friends, and even pastors may eventually wonder why the victim doesn't just leave the past in the past. Most victims long to do just that but are not able to do so. The lasting effects of sexual abuse are real, persistent, and often overwhelming. Indeed, just listing the effects can seem overwhelming. To prove a particular point, the following list is provided along with an invitation to the reader to read it from start to finish without interruption.

ENDURING PROBLEMS

In their 1992 publication *Healing the Wounds of Childhood: The Resource Guide for Adult Survivors of Childhood Abuse and Addictions,* D. A. Sexton, D. Tarter, and K. Gunn included a list of thirty-three long-term effects of sexual abuse.[1] Their list includes: guilt or shame; sense of isolation; depression; deep-seated anger or hostility; suicidal thoughts; obsessive-compulsive behaviors; emotional numbing; dependency or control in relationships; learned helplessness; low self-esteem; inability to play; flat affect; tendency toward being self-abusive; inability to trust; tendency toward victimization; denial; short-term relationships (lack of long-term commitment); fear of intimacy; immature emotions; generalized fear and anxiety; loss of memory about parts of childhood; grief over lost childhood; gravitating toward or creating chaos; constant flashbacks; feeling like "damaged goods"; sleep disturbances; somatic illness; dissociation ("spacing out" for significant periods of time without having a seizure); gender confusion; phobias; sexualized behaviors; becoming adult victims of sexual assault; and sexual maladjustment.

Although not all these effects have been documented by empirical studies,[2] in my clinical experience they are commonly observable in varying degrees among sexual abuse victims. Clinical experience also indicates that physical difficulties associated with sexual abuse can include pregnancy; sexually transmitted diseases; repeated urinary tract infections (often beginning at an early age); genital pain, bleeding, or itching; and difficulty walking. Behavioral difficulties may include eating disorders (overeating, bulimia, or anorexia); inappropriate involvement or preoccupation with sex; sex play with toys or objects; abuse of animals; fear of touch, home, or people; wearing a lot of clothing irrespective of the weather; public or excessive masturbation; sexual dysfunction; no sexual desire or promiscuity; drug or alcohol abuse or dependency; self-mutilation; irrational fears; and panic attacks.

Mental health professionals who encounter clients who keep their history of sexual abuse secret will likely diagnose either a borderline personality disorder, bipolar or unipolar depression, or post-traumatic stress disorder (the last diagnosis being most correct).

A PARTICULAR POINT

Now the readers are invited to gauge their own internal reactions to this daunting list. Many may find it difficult to hold all these symptoms in their minds at one time. Some may feel a sense of confusion, oppression, and chaos. If a reader is a victim of sexual abuse, she or he may feel a strong recognition of herself or himself in the list, but probably also feel greatly unsettled. These feelings give a hint to what it is like inside a victimized life. In short, living in the heart, mind, and soul of a sexual abuse victim is a chaotic, often nearly psychotic experience. (In the extreme, multiple severe experiences of sexual abuse at a very early age may result in what was once called multiple personality disorder and which the *DSM-IV* now calls dissociative identity disorder.)

Many victims and those who love them not only recognize the presence of many of the symptoms, but also continually question why these symptoms are present. Further, there is justifiable concern about what will become of the victim who exhibits a debilitating collection of symptoms.

PATHS OF DESTRUCTION

One possible result of sexual abuse is that the victims embark on a journey of self-defeat and self-destruction. Believing somehow that they deserved the abuse that was visited upon them, victims may feel unworthy of anything good or pleasurable. As a result, they may deny themselves good things and may consciously or unconsciously sabotage their own efforts to be successful in life. Some victims engage in what psychologists call a repetition compulsion. This means that they reenact the sexual abuse (usually finding someone to victimize them, but in a few cases becoming sexually abusive) with the unconscious wish that the experience will have a different result. Likewise, unusual or promiscuous sexual behavior may be another unconscious attempt by sexual abuse victims to correct their past.

It is important for all who care about sexual abuse victims truly to understand what is meant by the word "unconscious." Even though it is a word commonly used, "unconscious" has a specific clinical meaning that affects how we understand the sexual abuse victim. Human behavior is typically the result of our conscious thoughts, plans, and intentions. On the other hand, our behaviors can also be influenced or even driven by urges, feelings, and intentions of which we are not consciously aware. What this means is that sexual abuse victims may engage in many unreasonable or unwise behaviors without really knowing why. If questioned about why they terminated a good relationship, why they seem to "blow up" their own efforts at success, why they risked being sexually abused again, why they engaged in a particular sexual behavior, and so on, the victim who has not had therapy may have no rational reply.

As previously mentioned, sexual abuse is a trauma that may produce post-traumatic stress disorder (PTSD). Victims of this disorder (such as war veterans or survivors of the 9/11 terrorist attacks) may experience nightmares, flashbacks, unexplained physical sensations, paranoia, delusions about others, or other symptoms that may appear psychotic. Fortunately, the prognosis for recovery from PTSD (when properly diagnosed and treated) can be better than the prognosis for psychotic illness (for example, we can't cure schizophrenia). But before victims understand their disorder and how it relates to their sexual abuse, they frequently believe that they are "going crazy" and are reticent to tell anyone about their symptoms. Having experienced exceptional danger, victims also seldom feel safe anywhere and will often read danger or criticism into most situations, even if there is no danger or criticism.

Since sexual abuse is experienced as a severe trauma by many victims, victims may get through the experience by using what is called dissociation. If one has ever lost track of time and where he or she is while driving a long familiar stretch of road (usually driving while thinking intently about something else), then one has had the experience of dissociating. Dissociation means that even though one is physically engaged in an activity, that person is no longer conscious of the activity and often is not even conscious of bodily sensations. Dissociation is often a "God send" for persons who are sexually abused because they successfully go somewhere else with their conscious mind and shut out the abuse.

Unfortunately, some sexual abuse victims lose control of when, how often, or for how long they will dissociate (hence the potential to develop dissociative identity disorder). Even if a disorder does not develop, the victim may lose conscious access to memories of the abuse, grasping only memory fragments during flashbacks or nightmares. The lack of a coherent memory of the event may cause serious problems to the victim, both legally and socially. If victims begin to dissociate, they often describe to therapists the feeling that they are "no longer real." The sense of not being real is likely the result of being emotionally numb and feeling like one is outside of one's body, both of which are common to dissociation. Self-mutilation is common in these circumstances. The victim compulsively inflicts non-life-threatening cuts somewhere on the body (usually places easily concealed with clothing such as arms or legs or even breasts) to prove to oneself that he or she can still feel things and is still real.

Depression, self-mutilation, and the excessive need for safety may cause a victim to isolate oneself from others or may be a torturous source of continual shame. Since sexual boundaries have been grossly violated, the victim may react to the violation by either denying oneself any sexual activity or engaging in inappropriate activity. Lack of sexual activity (especially if the victim is married), promiscuity, or unusual sexual practices may contribute to feelings of shame or even a sense of sinfulness in victims.

In addition to being traumatic, the experience of sexual abuse represents an ultimate loss of physical control to victims. As a result, eating disorders (such as anorexia nervosa, bulimia, or compulsive overeating) may be unconscious attempts by victims to somehow soothe themselves and to gain control of at least one aspect of their lives (namely, what and how much they eat).

Unlike self-mutilation, which is not typically meant to be suicidal (but which may be an accidental result), suicidal intentions connected with depression may besiege the victims. Since they have been victimized, they may well enter into more passive attempts, rather than active attempts, at suicide. Sexual abuse victims are probably less likely to die by hanging themselves or shooting themselves, and more likely to die because they failed to take treatment for serious illness—failed to protect themselves, having put themselves into a dangerous situation—or from an "accidental" overdose of medications.

The enduring pain of sexual abuse and post-traumatic stress disorder (PTSD) that often follows frequently make life seem unbearable to victims. If they do not use dissociation to numb themselves to the pain (and sometimes even if they do use it), victims often use and abuse substances as "emotional anesthetics." Unfortunately, their problems can then be compounded by addiction. In these cases, intervention for addiction or substance abuse must often precede any intervention related to the abuse, or the victim will continue to use substances and confound therapy.

Though I know of no sexual abuse victim displaying all of the destructive behaviors listed above, all of these symptoms, disorders, and maladaptive behaviors have been observed in different sexual abuse victims. Untreated, the victims may lead tortured, lonely lives, often alienating themselves from the very people who care about them.

SURVIVAL AND THE PROCESS OF HEALING

So they approached Joseph, saying, "Your father gave this instruction before he died, 'Say to Joseph: I beg you, forgive the crime of your brothers and the wrong they did in harming you.' Now therefore please forgive the crime of the servants of the God of your father." Joseph wept when they spoke to him. Then his brothers also wept, fell down before him, and said, "We are here as your slaves." But Joseph said to them, "Do not be afraid! Am I in the place of God? Even though you intended to do harm to me, God intended it for good, in order to preserve a numerous people, as he is doing today." (Genesis 50:16-20)

As with Joseph, who experienced traumatic (though not sexual)[3] abuse from his brothers, the victims of sexual abuse may be able to cease being victims and become survivors instead. The passage at the end of Genesis is truly a remarkable paradigm for survival and spiritual healing from sexual abuse.

Ironically, the first thing victims are sometimes confronted with—the spiritual mandate to forgive—is often the last thing they are able to do. Like repentance, forgiveness is a *process* rather than a single *act*. Hebrew scholars will note that to repent means "to turn." The person who repents *turns from* one thing and *turns toward* another. But how often does a sex abuser turn from the offense and turn toward the one harmed to ask forgiveness? One could venture to say that without repentance, there is little hope of forgiveness.

How can one extend forgiveness to someone who never acknowledges a need to receive it? Instead, the sexual abuse victim frequently struggles with a spiritual mandate to give forgiveness in the absence of repentance. The image is one in which the abuser is still turned toward the act (justifying it somehow) with his or her back turned toward the victim. It is not unlike the image of our Christian God holding out forgiveness to a people who will not turn their attention *from* their sin, *toward* God. In the Joseph story, the brothers begin the process by repenting and asking for forgiveness. In reality, few sex abusers ever ask for forgiveness, although doing so could be positively therapeutic for the victim. In the Joseph story, the victim does not respond immediately with superficial forgiveness. Instead, forgiveness is recognized as being the purview more of God than of the victim ("Am I in the place of God?" Joseph asks). Indeed, Joseph becomes a survivor instead of a victim when he is able to take a broad view, looking to the future for the power and triumph of God, rather than attempting to do God's job of judging or forgiving his brothers.

Victims become survivors when they face their trauma (usually in therapy) and make some sense of their whole lives, including the sexual abuse. Often sexual abuse survivors can then use their experience of trauma to empathize with other trauma victims and use their increased awareness and intense need of safety to protect others vigilantly. Eventually, the sexual abuse becomes *one of* the important events of their lives rather than *the defining moment* of their existence. Healing often begins with forgiveness, not of the abuser, but of the victim's own self. Victims must often forgive themselves for believing false things, for treating themselves poorly, and for behaving inappropriately. They need to understand themselves and how they have behaved in the context of the trauma they have suffered. They may also need to ask forgiveness of and make amends to others possibly harmed by their behaviors who were not their abusers.

Eventually, they must, like Joseph, stop wishing to be God and give up trying to understand, fix, judge, or change the persons who abused them. The victims must reconcile themselves to the possibility that no matter how willing they may be to forgive their abusers, the abusers may never receive that forgiveness. And like Joseph, the survivors must weep and mourn all that was lost or taken from them.

Then the survivors can look forward instead of back, in faith that God can confound evil and bring out good (as God did for Joseph and as God did in the resurrection of Jesus Christ after crucifixion). It is God who can turn upside down (confound) the hideous experience of sexual abuse and bring from it something good. Like Joseph's brothers, the abusers may have meant it for harm, but God can use it for good. This theology can be tricky if misinterpreted. God is not the source of the evil, nor does God will the evil in the lives of those victimized. Humans will the evil act and possess the evil intention. But God is the transforming power that confounds the evil and, in spite of the evil intention, brings good instead.

A warning should be heeded by well-intentioned pastors or caregivers at this point. The process of healing is a long and slow one. It has many dimensions: physical, psychological, and spiritual. And though it may be easy for one who was never victimized to accept the theology offered above, for victims who are becoming survivors, the process is slow and frequent repetition is required. Survivors may apprehend part of or the entire spiritual dimension of healing and then lose it over and over again. Sexual abuse affects how one thinks and processes information. The chaos induced to mind, body, and spirit means the person may be lucid one moment, and at peace, but afraid or full of rage the next.

A sexual abuse victim may unconsciously be trying to prove that he or she is bad enough to deserve the abuse experienced. As a result, the victim may repeatedly do things to drive others away. When others are driven away, the victim not only confirms his or her own "badness," but often feels safer. The task of pastors and loved ones becomes that of tolerating the changes, sustaining the message of unconditional love, and being sensitive to the person's extreme need for safety. It is often the job of a therapist (rather than a pastor or a loved one) to help the victim confront the abuse and be a "container" for the victim's rage, shame, guilt, and fear so that the victim may become a survivor. Everyone in the victim/survivor's life, however, can serve to reassure the person (by keeping him or her in touch with reality) that the present is different, safer, and more genuinely loving than the past.

Given the description of sexual abuse victims above, one understands the challenge associated with loving and ministering to the victims. In the book *Pastoral Care for Survivors of Family Abuse,* James Leehan lists some victims' behaviors that "try the patience of a saint."[4] His list echoes the repeated (even if unspoken) questions (posed here in my words) in the lives of victims. "If I connect with you, will you approve of me and love me (as victims enter into all sorts of relationships, positive and negative, simply to prove to themselves that they are lovable)?" "Can I ever be 'bad' enough that you will stop loving me (as victims are constantly testing, sometimes with outrageous behaviors, whether the persons they love still love them)?" "Can I be the one who is in charge (since sexual abuse represents the loss of all control, the victims may try to control everything through manipulation)?" "Who is here, and are they mad at me or dangerous to me (as victims, for survival, seem always to be gauging the emotional state of those near them to keep themselves safe)?" "Are things too quiet; do I need to 'shake things up' (since the interior lives of victims are so chaotic, they may create chaos to feel 'normal')?" "What did you mean by that (since victims may view the actions of others through the lens of their past abuse and impute negative intentions to benign or even benevolent acts by others, they may react inappropriately)?"

Although the experience may try one's patience, understanding the reason for a victim's behavior usually helps pastors and loved ones tolerate and forgive the victim more easily.

MOST RULES HAVE EXCEPTIONS

There was a member of a congregation who experienced sexual abuse once at the hands of her father. The incident was discovered quickly. She was assured that the abuse was not her fault, and successful efforts kept her safe throughout the rest of her childhood. She spoke freely and confidentially to her (then divorced) mother about the sexual abuse and never saw her father alone again. She exhibited almost none of the problems listed above. Unfortunately, her daughter was left alone with the abuser by extended family members (unbeknownst to the mother), and the daughter was sexually abused. A couple of reasons were given for the mistake. First, the incident with the mother was so well handled that she was the exception to the rule and recovered quickly from the sexual abuse; hence, the incident was largely forgotten by the extended family. Second, the woman's father, her daughter's grandfather, was quite old, and the extended family believed his age would prevent future abuse.

5

Ministry With Victims, Abusers, and Their Families

*And he took them up in his arms, laid his hands on
them, and blessed them. (Mark 10:16)*

As a pastor, it can feel especially good to take a Sunday
off and attend a service where someone else does the
preaching for a change. Of course, listening to someone else can invite rather odious and even un-Christian com-
parisons to oneself. On one such Sunday, in a church far
from my home church, I listened to a sermon that was part
of a series on the Ten Commandments. This particular sermon dealt with the dictate to "honor thy father and thy
mother." Since I was working at the time with incest victims,
I was greatly troubled that no mention was made of what it
meant to "honor" one's father if, for any variety of reasons,
one's father did not appear to "merit" that honor. Later, the
pastor allowed a time of "free-spoken" prayer by the congregation, and I prayed aloud for victims of incest to discern
what it meant for them to honor their fathers.

The pastor spoke to me after service, grateful for my
prayer, but troubled. He knew that a family in the congregation had just received a foster child who was an incest
victim and that family (along with the child) was present at
worship. The pastor felt reticent to mention "difficult" parents in his sermon for fear of underscoring the child's
problem. But he agreed that something should have been
said. Then the foster family approached me and thanked me

for my prayer, noting how upset their foster daughter was during the sermon, and how much better she seemed to be after the prayer.

Ministry is composed of so many dimensions (worship, sacrament, teaching, preaching, community-building, pastoral care, emergency and bereavement support, and so on) that it becomes difficult to attend to every aspect of a situation at all times. When an event as serious as sexual abuse occurs among a worship community, most leaders will attend to the hurt in a letter, sermon, counseling session, or some other way (as long as the leaders understand that the whole community has, in fact, been affected). A Roman Catholic woman expressed well the dilemma facing those who would minister in this era when sexual abuse is known and visible in our communities of faith. She noted that the victim of sexual abuse, though clearly the one who is most harmed, is not really the only victim. Any time the loving act of sex is defiled by abuse, the abuse tears at the fabric of the entire community. And especially when the abuser is a church leader, the whole church is victimized.

But in what way should church staff be mindful of sexual abuse victims (and abusers!) who are a part of their congregation in the day-to-day conduct of ministry? There are ways to be mindful without being obsessive about the problem. Awareness based on sound clinical information (such as this book attempts to provide) can inform a pastor's, teacher's, or staff's work. This chapter is offered, based upon experience in churches with sexual abuse victims and survivors, to highlight concerns specific to daily ministry.

THEOLOGY AND ABUSE

As noted in chapter 1, some theological concepts, if taken at face value, may be very troubling to sexual abuse victims. Whether faced with Paul's discussion of "conjugal rights" in his first letter to the Corinthians or the Roman Catholic

Church's statement about "irrevocable personal consent" in the conjugal covenant, great sensitivity is called for in discussions with victims. One anonymous author,[1] whose father (a church elder) sexually abused his sister, urges against "theological orthodoxy" without "equally deep commitment to holiness of life."

But less obvious theological difficulties frequently plague the spiritual lives of victims. Since sexual abuse can be severely traumatic, victims may view most every aspect of life through the lens of that trauma. The "lens of trauma" can distort the original intention of seemingly benign theological ideas. What does it mean that God is a father (Abba, daddy) if one's own father was sexually abusive? What kind of father loves the world so much that he sends his own son to die? Is that some sort of cosmic child abuse? What is the meaning of suffering and hope, and should one be thankful for the suffering that comes from abuse? Who is this God who has a plan for our lives but allows sexual abuse? Isn't God paying attention? Was the abuse part of God's plan?

Imagine the following psalm as it might be heard by the victim of sexual abuse whose abuser violated him, day or night, wherever he went as a child.

> Where can I go from your spirit?
>   Or where can I flee from your presence?
> If I ascend to heaven, you are there;
>   if I make my bed in Sheol, you are there.
> If I take the wings of the morning
>   and settle at the farthest limits of the sea,
> even there your hand shall lead me,
>   and your right hand shall hold me fast.
> If I say, "Surely the darkness shall cover me,
>   and the light around me become night,"
> even the darkness is not dark to you;
>   the night is as bright as the day,
>   for darkness is as light to you. (Psalm 139:7-12)

These words about the persistent faithfulness of a loving

God, meant to be of greatest comfort, can instead be interpreted by a sexual abuse victim as indicative of the hopeless struggle to escape the darkness of their lives. There is no where to flee; they will always be held fast.

In frustration, pastors have asked, "Do I have to make abuse an issue for everything I preach or teach? Am I caught in a stranglehold because what I say may offend someone?" The answer, of course, is no. If, rather than being *directed* by the struggles of sexual abuse victims, one's theological discussions are *informed* by them, then often a single sentence can both address concerns and add richness to the discussion. Perhaps it is especially important for victims, whose lives may have been governed by bad secrets and a family conspiracy of silence, to feel that at last they are heard and their plight is named when sermons or teachings at least mention their circumstances. Frequently, the questions associated with abuse are similar to those being asked by persons whose lives have included some other kind of suffering anyway. Sometimes all that is called for in a theological discussion is reiteration of what is actually meant in order to avoid distortion by a victim.

One need not always directly reference sexual abuse at these times (although doing so occasionally will signal to abuse victims that the speaker is someone who can tolerate a discussion with abuse victims at another time). One can simply acknowledge times when applying the theology to one's life can be more complicated, such as when others do harm to your life. Such a statement is a sign that victims' life experiences have been taken into account and are not once again ignored or discounted.

THE PROBLEM OF LANGUAGE AND SYMBOLS

Since faith and the spiritual journey of any person are intangible, language and symbols are hallmarks of religious life. Like theology, language and symbols can be misinterpreted or distorted. But also like theology, it is often untenable to the practice of faith simply to discard important language or symbols.

As an alternative, one can recognize the pain experienced in certain language or symbols and either offer helpful alternatives or work to reclaim the old language and symbol as something positive. For example, the symbol of God as Father can be expanded to include the female images of God (for example, the feminine noun Spirit—*ruach,* in Hebrew). In addition, the nature of "Fatherhood" demonstrated by God, as opposed to that demonstrated by any of us who are human fathers, can likewise be highlighted to help reclaim the symbol.

Language referring to humans can easily be made inclusive instead of exclusive. Though inclusive language has become a standard for written work, many persons in religious communities still adamantly reject what they view as a "ridiculous" practice. Typically the argument against inclusive language suggests that "it doesn't make any difference" and that the speaker has no desire to be "politically correct." For a girl or woman who has been sexually abused by a man, the difference between male and female has been made palpably clear. If God came to save all *men,* then they, as females, may well not feel included. Indeed, these girls and women may not "feel saved," especially since it already seems as if God did not save them from the abuse or the problems that followed it. Clearly to these victims, the use of inclusive language is not about political correctness.

If someone insists that inclusive language "doesn't matter," they should use inclusive language by all means. Since the use of inclusive language does not matter to the speaker or writer, but the use of exclusive language can be hurtful to others, why would a caring Christian choose otherwise than to be inclusive?

THE BIBLE: HURTING AND HEALING

Several examples have already been given of how Scripture can be used to harm instead of help. This practice is as old as the Gospels. One need only point to the temptation of Jesus in the fourth chapter of Matthew's Gospel to see how the "devil" used Scripture to try to lead the Messiah astray.

Unfortunately, Scripture can also be unwittingly used to hurt rather than to heal, if not carefully interpreted. Biblical references to forgiving others,[2] submitting to one's husband,[3] honoring one's parent, disciplining one's children,[4] patiently enduring suffering (in silence),[5] avoiding divorce, and so on, can be very hurtful to sexual abuse victims if they are quickly "glossed over" rather than carefully discussed.

On the other hand, Scripture can also provide an excellent source for recovery and healing if used well with sexual abuse victims (and with others who have endured great suffering in life). The brief application of the Joseph story in the previous chapter is only one such example. The following samples are offered to encourage further exploration by pastors and others seeking to plumb the Bible for its therapeutic richness.

EXAMPLES OF USING THE BIBLE FOR HEALING

Often an understanding of biblical texts can assist victims of sexual abuse (or of any abuse) in their healing and recovery efforts. But as the previous section noted, the use of biblical passages out of context, or when presented as "platitudes," can be painful to victims or may at least be heard by victims as someone telling them "just to get over it." The following are "samples" (rather than "examples") of how Scripture may be used *in the context of a larger discussion* with victims to assist them in their spiritual, emotional, and psychological healing. Many other texts would likely serve as well. These are some samples presented in the context of a victim's particular struggle that may be appropriated by caring pastors or staff. If texts are simply "delivered" and not discussed in the context of the victim's real life, the victim may experience the texts as merely "quick bandages" on "gaping open wounds."

One might assure victims that it is reasonable for them to turn to God. Although Scripture does *not* say, "God helps them who help themselves"; it says instead, "My help comes from the Lord, who made heaven and earth" [Ps. 121:2]; and "The LORD helps them and rescues them; [the LORD] rescues them from the wicked, and saves them, because they take refuge in (the LORD)" (Ps. 37:40).

Since most victims of sexual abuse eventually believe they are so valueless that they deserve the abuse, one should not underestimate the power of the biblical texts that refute that notion. As Scripture begins, God pronounces humans to be "very good" creations, created in the very image of the creator (Gen. 1:27-31). Not only is it true that God does not create "junk" (as many sexual abuse victims believe themselves to be), but also later, the writer of the first letter of John writes: "See what love the Father has given us, that we should be called children of God; and that is what we are" (3:1).

Affirming a victim's value as an actual "child of God" denies any notion that something makes the victim deserving of abuse.

When a victim realizes that she or he really did not deserve the sexual abuse, she or he often (understandably) feels very angry about the abuse. Many victims fear the depth of the rage they feel. In fact, it is a good idea for them to express that rage in the safety, confidentiality, and therapeutic process of therapy. Instead of expressing it appropriately, victims often try to deny or disregard their rage. Spiritual persons may well add some "religious" excuse for not addressing the anger they feel. For them, Paul's direction to "*be angry* but do not sin" (Eph. 4:26, emphasis mine) may come as a surprise. Paul's advice to "be angry" may not "feel" right, but it is psychologically sound. Unfortunately, some persons who try to avoid their rage about their abuse find the anger escaping toward others besides the abuser. These angry expressions may be very hard for victims to control until they confront their rage (appropriately in therapy) with regard to their sexual abuse. In a private correspondence with me, Dr. Dan Bagby (editor of this book), noted the helpful distinction between two Greek words used in the New Testament that are both translated as the English word "anger." The first, *thumos*, used in this Pauline passage, refers to "the passion of the moment, often elicited by an injustice, abuse or wrong." The other Greek word used elsewhere in the New Testament for anger, *orge*, refers to "the destructive sinful kind: a nurtured, encouraged, and sustained anger—so as to will harm by ongoing premeditation."[6]

Perhaps some of the confusion comes from the use of a single word, "anger," without recognizing the source of the emotion. In *The Enigma of Anger*, Garret Keizer (an Episcopal priest) distinguishes anger by type.[7] Having discussed anger as resulting from fear, or from grief, or from a sense of privilege (all of which may lead to sin) he dares to discuss "anger as grace." Lifting up the paradoxical image of Moses literally "breaking the law" by smashing the tablets in anger, Keizer writes:

> The action amounts to an eleventh commandment: Thou shalt break the law itself for the sake of righteousness. . . . For better or for worse, it serves as a justification for anger. . . . Like a wife finally angry enough to pull off her wedding ring in the face of abuse.[8]

Anger at someone who has harmed you (such as a sexual abuser) is normal and a frequent complaint offered to God in the psalms:

> Hear my voice, O God, in my complaint;
> preserve my life from the dread enemy.
> Hide me from the secret plots of the wicked,
> from the scheming of evil doers. (Ps. 64:1-2)

> Out of the depths I cry to you, O LORD.
> Lord, hear my voice!
> Let your ears be attentive
> to the voice of my supplications!
> (Ps. 130:1-2)

The psalms also provide a model of human longing and impatience, often shared by victims, in the face of the apparent "silence" of God after they have voiced their complaint.

> "How long, O LORD? Will you forget me forever?
>   How long will you hide your face from me?
> How long must I bear pain in my soul,
>   and have sorrow in my heart all day long?
> How long shall my enemy be exalted over me?" (Ps. 13:1-2)

An additional source of discomfort for sexual abuse victims (and others who have experienced great hardship in life) is their honest anger at God. Victims often feel ashamed or even sinful for feeling anger at God and would never think of expressing that anger (as if God is not strong enough or loving enough or understanding enough or forgiving enough to bear the victim's rage). But Scripture holds examples of just that sort of anger expressed to a God who was tough enough and compassionate enough to take it. Job, who did nothing wrong but suffered much, makes one such complaint:

> "Why are times not kept by the Almighty,
>   and why do those who know him never see his days?. . .
> From the city the dying groan,
>   and the throat of the wounded cries for help;
>   yet God pays no attention to their prayer." (Job 24:1, 12)

Pastors and others may wish to rush to the good news that God consistently provides in response to these angry complaints. But it is commonly more therapeutic for sexual abuse victims (as it was therapeutic to those who wrote the complaints) to *voice their pain* before rushing to God's response. Indeed, pastors would do especially well to refer victims, who are "getting in touch" with their anger without therapy, for therapy as soon as possible. This phase of the healing process can be protracted and the victims very volatile. Without therapy, victims may become suicidal. Even with therapy, they may experience deep depression.

Following an appropriately long period of anger (which victims may revisit from time to time in the future), victims may be receptive to hearing about the response of God to their cries of pain. As previously mentioned, when one instills a genuine hope for the future, a large portion of healing is accomplished. Both the power of God to triumph over the evil of their past (*"Sing to the* LORD, *for [the* LORD] *has triumphed gloriously"* [Exod. 15:21]) and God's tender care (*And he took them up in his arms, laid his hands on them, and blessed them* [Mark 10:16]) may be shared.

With enough healing, survivors may be encouraged to take risks with God and with others. One may use the portent of the woman and the dragon from Revelation chapter 12 allegorically at this time. As victims seek to give birth to a new, more trusting life, they may well fear that the "dragon" of their past sits in wait to devour the new life. But God is faithful. The new life (the newborn baby) is snatched from the "dragon's" mouth. Next, the personified new life is seen sitting safely with God. Meanwhile the mother (allegorically, a victim's past) escapes and is nourished by God (rather than forgotten or destroyed).

The God who protects and nourishes is not a capricious divinity. One need only point again to the psalms to illustrate this point. God has been faithful not in word alone or only sporadically. God has established a history of action that proves him to be both genuinely loving and trustworthy. Over the history recounted in Psalm 105 and Psalm 136, God earns our trust through divine acts of creation and through God's faithfulness toward Abraham, Isaac, Jacob, Joseph, and Moses. Beyond the Psalms, the stories of Scripture reassure us of God's trustworthiness through the establishment of God's church. Since safety and trust are paramount issues to victims and survivors, the trustworthiness of God, even in the face of apparent evil or defeat is a key to spiritual healing and health. God's trustworthiness is a primary reason to have hope.

Finally, questions of forgiveness may be addressed if the survivor is able to tolerate the discussion. The comments about forgiveness and the use of the Joseph story presented in the last chapter may help at this time.

Every tradition develops its own method to understand Scripture. Whatever the tradition, one may be confident that, used appropriately, the Bible can be an excellent resource for spiritual healing and health for sexual abuse victims (and for their families as well).

MINISTRY TO ABUSERS

Ministers do not always have free choice of the recipients to whom God calls them to minister. Some of us are called to minister to those who are sexually abusive. In fact, all of us who do ministry are in contact with people who are, in some way, abusive (though not necessarily sexually abusive), even if we don't know it. In each case, our work may be enlightened by the anonymous author cited previously who writes the following about his sexually abusive father (who was also a church leader):

> My father somehow compartmentalized his theology and his ethics. Dad was superb in theological debates. . . . But we always felt that there was a disconnect between what he *said* and what he *did*.[9]

Both clinical and pastoral experience suggests that the "disconnect" between theology and behavior is typical in sexual abusers (and often a hallmark of most sinful behavior). This "compartmentalization" gives the pretense of individual integrity despite one's behavior and occurs in many situations. One needs only to think about Christians who lie on their income tax forms while asking the pious church-going sexual abuser, "How can you do that?" A psychologist may even point out that if the "compartmentalization" is strong enough (that is, there is a "solid wall" separating the person's theology for their consideration of their actual behavior), the abuser may genuinely believe the theology he or she expounds.

In any case, when working with known sexual offenders, the following suggestions may guide pastoral care:

Be safe—If the minister questions his or her own safety with the abuser, make arrangements to assure safety.

Listen to yourself—Not every minister is well suited to this sort of ministry. Don't expect more of yourself than you can reasonably tolerate or deliver since doing so will not serve you or the abuser well.

Set clear limits, and expect them to be tested—The violation of boundaries (even nonsexual limits) is a hallmark of sexual abusers. Every boundary violation should be explicitly noted out loud since boundary violation of any kind begins the process toward reoffending.

Discuss consequences for behavior in positive terms as a means of "discipline"—That is, as both a means to learn (disciple) and as a "spiritual discipline" for God to reform the abuser's life.

Talk about trust—Especially help the abuser understand that regaining trust should not be automatic (like "cheap grace"), but a process in which the former abuser slowly *earns* trust by demonstrating appropriate behavior over a long period of time.

Instill hope—Just as hope is extended over time to victims, hope in the context of forgiving love can be extended to abusers, but not in the absence of boundaries and "discipline."

FOR FAMILIES

Ministry to family and friends of both those who abuse and those who are abusers comes effectively in two forms:

- Help family and friends know what to expect and how to understand abusers and those whom they abuse.
- Be compassionate and voice the struggle family and friends must be enduring themselves through this journey.

PASTORAL CARE

Pastoral care must be conducted with concern for safety first, and for confidentiality second. For abusers, safety involves the pastor and those in the church who may have continued contact with the abuser. For victims, providing safety means attending to the victim's sense of what it takes to feel safe, rather than any "rational" measures. If victims need to sit in a chair by a door (for "quick escape") or with their backs to a wall (so no one can sneak up on them) in order to feel safe, then they should do so. It does not matter that they will have no need for escape or that no one will sneak up on them. If they need to meet in a public place, then do so, but be aware of confidentiality during the meeting.

Confidentiality should be discussed explicitly. Everything that is not an immediate danger to self or others should remain absolutely confidential unless it involves new knowledge of child abuse, which must be reported. As regards danger to self and others, pastoral counselors should not shy away from asking those in their care if they are planning to harm anyone. Hospitalization should be sought immediately (and without debate) if the person plans to harm himself or herself or others.

Notwithstanding the theology and information shared earlier in this book, pastoral care in these circumstances more often means "sitting with people and their pain" rather than "solving a problem" or "giving an answer." Especially with victims, the person receiving care should set the pace for what they can hear or tolerate from the pastor.

Above all, pastoral care should not invite caregivers to forget who is God and who is not. Needless to say, prayer (not lectures) has, at times, been more effective than human efforts at healing. Prayer, coupled with a sustained commitment to stay with the person in need, offers a powerful formula for change.

REFERRAL SOURCES

Knowing the limits of our competence is as important as competent ministry. Referral sources specific to sexual abuse may be obtained in several ways. One may contact the American Psychological Association and ask for therapists specializing in trauma and abuse in the area (www.apa.org). Likewise those names may be obtained by contacting the state's psychological association. Social workers and other mental health professionals may be provided by the state's Department of Human Services, or they may direct the caller to a referral source. Finally, both the American Association of Pastoral Counselors (AAPC) and the American Association of Marriage and Family Therapists (AAMFT) may also provide contact with professionals trained to deal with trauma and abuse (www.aamft.org and www.aapc.org).

An organization called ChildHelp offers a national hotline to report any sort of child abuse at 1-800-4-A-Child (1-800-422-4453).[10] Some states may not have twenty-four-hour hotlines. The national hotline seeks to be a backup if for any reason one cannot report an allegation of child abuse to Department of Human Services hotline in the state in which the abuse allegedly occurred. The following is a list of abuse hotlines, by state, updated at the time of this book's publication.

Alabama	Report by county 334-242-9500
Alaska	907-269-3900 (if calling from out of state)
	800-478-4444 (if calling from in state) or Division of Family and Youth Services Regional Office
Arizona	888-SOS-CHILD (888-767-2445)
Arkansas	800-482-5964
California	Report by county
	916-445-2832 (out of state)
Colorado	Report by county
	303-866-3003 (nationwide)
Connecticut	800-842-2288 (nationwide)
	800-624-5518 (TDD/hearing impaired, in state)
Delaware	800-292-9582
	302-577-6550 (out of state)
District of Columbia	202-671-7233 (nationwide)
Florida	800-962-2873 (nationwide)
Georgia	Report by county
Hawaii	Report by island 808-832-5300 (Oahu)
Idaho	Report by Regional Office
Illinois	800-252-2873 (in state)
	217-524-2606 (out of state)
Indiana	800-800-5556 (in state)
	Out of state, report by Regional Office
Iowa	800-362-2178 (nationwide)
Kansas	800-922-5330
	785-296-0044 (out of state)
Kentucky	800-752-6200
	502-595-4550 (out of state)
Louisiana	Report by parish/county
	225-342-6832 (out of state, during business hours)

103

Maine   800-452-1999
               207-287-2982 (out of state)
               201-287-3492 (TTY)
Maryland   800-332-6347 (in state)
               Out of state, report by county
Massachusetts 800-792-5200
               617-232-4882 (out of state)
Michigan   800-942-4357
               517-373-3572 (out of state)
Minnesota   Report by county
Mississippi   800-222-8000
               601-359-4991 (out of state)
Missouri   800-392-3738
               572-751-3448 (out of state)
Montana   800-332-6100
               406-444-5900 (out of state)
Nebraska   800-652-1999
               402-595-1324 (out of state, business hours only)
Nevada   800-992-5757
               775-684-4400 (out of state, business hours only)
New Hampshire   800-894-5533 (in state)
               800-852-3388 (in state, after hours)
               603-271-6563 (out of state)
               603-225-9000 (out of state, after hours)
New Jersey   800-792-8610 (nationwide, 24 hours)
               800-835-5510 (TDD/hearing impaired)
New Mexico   800-797-3260 (in state, 24 hours)
               505-841-6100 (out of state, 24 hours)
New York   800-342-3720
               518-474-8740 (out of state)
North Carolina   Report by county
North Dakota   Report by Regional Office
               701-328-2316 (nationwide, business hours only)
               800-245-3736 (in state, business hours only)

104

Ohio	Report by county
	614-466-9824 (nationwide, business hours only)
Oklahoma	800-522-3511 (nationwide, 24 hours)
Oregon	800-854-3508 ext. 2402 (in state, business hours)
	503-378-5414 (TTY, hearing impaired)
	503-378-6704 (nationwide, business hours)
Pennsylvania	800-932-0313 (in state)
	717-783-8744 (nationwide)
Rhode Island	800-RI-CHILD
	(800-742-4453) (nationwide, 24 hours)
South Carolina	Report by county (in state)
	803-898-7318 (out of state, business hrs.)
South Dakota	Report by county
	605-773-3227 (nationwide, business hours)
Tennessee	Report by county
	615-532-3545 (nationwide, business hours)
	After hours, contact Department of Human Services
Texas	800-252-5400
	512-834-3784 (out of state, business hours)
	512-832-2020 (out of state, after hours)
Utah	800-678-9399 (nationwide)
Vermont	Report by county during business hours
	800-649-5285 (in state)
Virginia	800-552-7096
	804-786-8536 (out of state)
	Or with Prevent Child Abuse Virginia at
	804-775-1777 or 1-800-CHILDREN
Washington	800-562-5624 (nationwide)
West Virginia	800-352-6513
	800-558-7980 (out of state, business hours)
Wisconsin	Report by county
	608-266-3036 (nationwide, business hours)
Wyoming	800-457-3659 (in state, report by county)

Epilogue
Sexual Shalom

Peace I leave with you; my peace I give to you. I do not give to you as the world gives. Do not let your hearts be troubled, and do not let them be afraid. (John 14:27)

And the peace of God, which surpasses all understanding, will guard your hearts and your minds in Christ Jesus. (Philippians 4:7)

In Israel, *shalom* is used both to greet and to say goodbye. The simplest translation of this Hebrew word, of course, is *peace*. But most pastors know that the term means much more than either "tranquillity" or "the absence or opposite of war." There is an approachable exposition of the word *shalom* and of its Greek counterpart *(eirene)* published by the Kerygma Bible Study group.[1] That study notes that *shalom* appears about 250 times in the Old Testament, and its meaning may include wholeness, health, harmony, or the completeness God intends for our world.

In her 1993 work, *Sexual Character*, Marva Dawn joins the biblical meaning of *shalom* to sexuality.[2] Though I may take issue with some of Dr. Dawn's application of the concept of "sexual shalom," I can hardly argue with her choice to combine these words, or with her longing for sexual shalom among women and men.

Dr. Dawn's application of the word *shalom* to a variety of human situations finds precedence in the biblical texts. For example, one translation of 2 Samuel 11:7 describes King David inquiring about the *shalom* of Joab, the *shalom* of the people, and the *shalom* of the war.[3] Understanding *shalom* to mean more than the typical English meaning for the word "peace," the king was asking about the health, wholeness, and completeness intended by God for Joab, the people, and even for the war. If King David can apply *shalom* to an event as destructive as war, one can easily support a yearning for *shalom* in sexuality.

If sexual shalom means sexual health, sexual harmony, and the sexual wholeness intended by God, then sexual shalom is what sexual abuse seeks to destroy primarily in the lives of its victims (and likely in the abusers' lives as well). On an emotional, physical, and spiritual level, sexual health is overcome with "dis-ease" (a profound lack of ease); sexual harmony is disrupted by relational discord; and sexual wholeness is overcome by chaotic fragmentation of the lives of those involved in sexual abuse. A pastoral response to sexual abuse requires, overall, whatever effort may be required to preserve and redevelop God's *shalom* to the sexual dimension of these people's lives.

Sexual abuse seeks to destroy sexual shalom for both the victim and the abuser and for the congregation that surrounds them as well. Nancy Myer Hopkins and her associates working with the Interfaith Sexual Trauma Institute in Collegeville, Minnesota, have explored the effect on congregations since Dr. Hopkins published "The Congregation Is Also a Victim" in 1992.[4] With the work of Edwin Friedman in 1985, many have recognized that a congregation's day-to-day functioning resembles the functioning of what psychologists call a "family system."[5] As a result, a catastrophic event (such as sexual abuse) affects the whole system (the functioning of the entire congregation), and not just the individuals who are directly involved in the abuse itself.

When the abuser is clergy, the effect on the family system of the congregation is perhaps most acute. Unsuspecting successors to clergy abusers, sometimes called "afterpastors"[6] often encounter peculiar patterns of congregational behavior (dynamics of the system) affected by the history of clergy sexual abuse, even several years after the event. Although one would do well to prevent or respond appropriately to sexual abuse to develop sexual shalom in the first place (the purpose and hope of this book), few pastors and congregations have consciously done so in the past. As a result, thankfully, resources are available to religious leaders who are faced with the daunting task of working with congregations whose histories include unresolved trauma caused by clergy sexual abuse.[7] Indeed, the need to recognize the lingering harm to sexual shalom in traumatized congregations is not limited to those congregations of which the abuser was clergy. In fact, none of us who pastor any such traumatized congregation after the event are really afterpastors, because the trauma is real and present and far from over until some semblance of sexual shalom is restored. As a result, providing a "pastoral response" to sexual abuse—restoring sexual shalom—is an awesome responsibility for those in ministry with a congregation, no matter when the abuse took place or by whom.

One important aspect of a discussion of sexual shalom that may be crucial to those whose ministries require a pastoral response to sexual abuse is to resist a view of sexual shalom as an ideal after which we yearn. It is indisputable that "perfect" sexual shalom will likely never be experienced outside the parousia. But it may be more helpful to understand sexual shalom as "more or less present on a continuum" rather than "perfectly present or absent." As the scriptures used to begin this epilogue note, the Messiah promised peace, a peace beyond our human understanding, as surely as the advocate was promised, to all who live on after the resurrection. Indeed, to celebrate the completeness, harmony, wholeness, and health that God intends, present in each person to whatever extent, is to honor the person as a "good creation of God" who sustains the *imago Dei* (image of God) no matter what trauma endured. Looking for the sexual shalom present in the lives of victims, abusers, and those who love them is to adopt a "competence" model of pastoral response (recognizing what is present *before* any emphasis on what is lacking), rather than the typical "deficit" model (trying to fix what is *wrong*) for pastoral care. Working together to "enhance and grow" the sexual shalom that remains in those involved in sexual abuse simultaneously ministers to their needs and denies the lie that they are any less the "children of God" proclaimed by Scripture.

This book sought to provide information that will assist us as we seek to enhance and grow the sexual shalom that remains in those touched by the trauma of sexual abuse. But it closes with a prayer for how we will use this information as well. The prayer is for openness: to broach the situation and deal with the issue. The prayer is that we might provide a consistent demonstration of our trustworthiness by setting and maintaining healthy personal boundaries and appropriate reactions to the actions of others. The prayer is that we might work to ensure safety for everyone, sensitivity to the complexities of sexual abuse, and sanctuary for all whose lives are threatened or ravaged by the experience of sexual abuse. Finally, it is a prayer that we might provide persistent and unconditional love, lifting up all that is good in God's creation, while we honestly recognize and respond to wounds that people can inflict upon one another. With this prayer comes the conviction that God's sexual shalom comes to us, as certainly as the rest of the Kingdom of God comes!

Notes

INTRODUCTION: LEVIATHAN

1. Elinor Burkett and Frank Bruni, *A Gospel of Shame: Children, Sexual Abuse, and the Catholic Church* (New York: Viking, 1993), 47.

2. Marie M. Fortune, *Violence in the Family: A Workshop Curriculum for Clergy and Other Helpers* (Cleveland: Pilgrim Press, 1991).

3. Judith Lewis Herman, *Father-Daughter Incest* (Cambridge, Mass.: Harvard University Press, 1981).

4. Specifically, in *Child Abuse and Neglect: Critical First Steps in Response to a National Emergency* (Washington, D.C.: Advisory Board on Child Abuse and Neglect, 1990), the U.S. Advisory Board on Child Abuse and Neglect wrote: "Although child maltreatment occurs in all socioeconomic and cultural groups in society, its reported incidence is disproportionately large within those groups that are least powerful and subjected to the most stressors" (p. 17). However, as noted in chapter 2 of this book, sexual abuse is not as connected to stress as is physical abuse.

5. Drawn from *Child Abuse and Neglect* and quoted in *Creating Caring Communities: Blueprint for an Effective Federal Policy on Child Abuse and Neglect* (U.S. Government Printing Office, 1991-526-132/ 40777, 1991), 61.

6. Made popular by the work of Irvin D. Yalom as one of the therapeutic factors in group psychotherapy (*The Theory and Practice of Group Psychotherapy,* 3rd ed. [New York: Basic Books, 1985] among other works by Yalom), psychological literature is replete with empirical studies of therapy efficacy and outcome that include "the installation of hope" as an important "therapeutic factor" in many different therapy situations.

7. From *Services for Occasions of Pastoral Care: The Worship of God* (Louisville, Ky.: Westminster/John Knox Press, 1990), 13 (emphasis added).

CHAPTER 1. THE NATURE OF SEXUAL ABUSE

1. See Marie Marshall Fortune, *Is Nothing Sacred? When Sex Invades the Pastoral Relationship* (San Francisco: Harper & Row, 1989), and reissued as *Is Nothing Sacred? The Story of a Pastor, the Women He Sexually*

Abused, and the Congregation He Nearly Destroyed (Cleveland, Ohio: United Church Press, 1999). It was the winner of the 1990 Book Award of the Year from the Academy of Parish Clergy.

2. See "US Bishops Affirm 'Zero Tolerance' Policy for Sex Abusers" (*Catholic World News* [among many others], 14 June 2002), at www.cwnews.com. In response, the Vatican raised significant questions regarding the policy and priests' rights to due process in a seven-paragraph response urging "further reflection and revision" of the policy. See "The Vatican Should Honor Thy Laity" (*Vatican Post*, 22 October 2002) at www.vaticanpost.com.

3. The content of the resolution passed in Columbus, Ohio, as reported in *The Layman*, vol. 35, no. 4 (August 2002): 9.

4. See Phyllis Trible, *Texts of Terror: Literary Feminist Readings of Biblical Narratives* (Philadelphia: Fortress Press, 1984).

5. See S. X. Radbill, "A History of Child Abuse and Infanticide" in *The Battered Child*, 2nd ed., ed. Ray E. Helfer and C. Henry Kempe ([Chicago: University of Chicago Press, 1974], 7-21); S. X. Radbill, "Children in a World of Violence: A History of Child Abuse" in *The Battered Child,* 4th ed., ed. Ray E. Helfer and C. Henry Kempe ([Chicago: University of Chicago Press, 1987], 3-21); and C. J. Ross, "The Lesson of the Past: Defining and Controlling Child Abuse in the United States" in *Child Abuse: An Agenda for Action*, ed. G. Gerbner, C. J. Ross, and E. Ziegler ([New York: Oxford University Press, 1980], 63-81); as well as my dissertation, "Engaging Neighborhoods: A Neighborhood-Based Strategy for the Primary Prevention of Child Maltreatment in the United States" (Widener University, 1999).

6. David Finkelhor, *Sexually Victimized Children* (New York: Free Press, 1979).

7. Fay's guide for talking with children was distributed by the King County Sexual Assault Resource Center in Seattle, Washington.

8. Florence Rush, *The Best Kept Secret: Sexual Abuse of Children* (New York: McGraw-Hill, 1981).

9. Judith Lewis Herman, *Father-Daughter Incest* (Cambridge: Harvard University Press, 1981).

10. Ellen Bass and Louise Thornton, eds., *I Never Told Anyone: Writing by Women Survivors of Sexual Child Abuse* (New York: Harper & Row, 1983).

11. Marie M. Fortune, *Sexual Violence: The Unmentionable Sin* (New York: Pilgrim Press, 1983).

12. Elinor Burkett and Grank Bruni, *Gospel of Shame: Children, Sexual Abuse, and the Catholic Church* (New York: Viking, 1993).

13. These are the first two definitions from *Webster's New Universal Unabridged Dictionary, Deluxe Second Edition* (New York: Simon and Schuster, 1983).

14. *Diagnostic and Statistical Manual of Mental Disorders* (Washington, D.C.: American Psychiatric Association, 1994).

15. Although the scenarios described in this book are based upon actual experiences, names, locations, and other identifying information have been changed to protect the privacy of others.

16. These terms are common among mental health professionals and can be found in a variety of books, including *Child Sexual Abuse: New Theory and Research* by D. Finkelhor (New York: Free Press, 1984); *By Silence Betrayed: Sexual Abuse of Children in America* by John Crewdson (Boston: Little, Brown, 1988); *Victims No Longer: Men Recovering from Incest and Other Sexual Child Abuse* by Mike Lew (New York: Harper & Row, 1990); and *The Courage to Heal: A Guide for Women Survivors of Child Sexual Abuse* by Ellen Bass and Laura Davis (New York: Harper & Row, 1988). There is not a distinction made between pedophilia and ephebophilia, however, in the *Diagnostic and Statistical Manual*, 4th ed. *(DSM-IV)*.

17. The following, taken from *Catechism of the Catholic Church*, 2nd ed. (Washington, D.C.: Libreria Editrice Vaticana, 1997), should be carefully and compassionately interpreted to victims of sexual abuse by their spouses: "The married couple forms 'the intimate partnership of life and love established by the Creator and governed by his laws; it is rooted in the *conjugal covenant*, that is, in their *irrevocable* personal consent.' Both give themselves definitely and totally to one another" (p. 568, emphasis added). Equal care and compassion should be exercised when interpreting 1 Corinthians 7:3ff., which discusses "conjugal rights" and the setting aside of those "rights."

18. Studies (especially in Canada with convicted sex offenders) demonstrate that the relationship of the abuser to the victim (family member, acquaintance, stranger) is directly related to the risk that he or she will abuse again. In these studies, a far greater number of sex offenders victimized persons related or known to them. (See *Static-99: Improving Actuarial Risk Assessments for Sex Offenders*, user report 99-02 [Ottawa: Department of the Solicitor General of Canada, 1999]; and *The Sex Offender Need Assessment Rating [SONAR]: A Method for Measuring Change in Risk Levels*, user report 00-01 [Ottawa: Department of the Solicitor General of Canada, 2000].)

19. See T. Barr, "E-Futures: Towards a Better Understanding of Internet Users" (2001), *Deakin Lectures*, at www.abc.net.au/rn/deakin/default.html.

20. See R. Starch, "The American Online/Roper Starch Youth Cyberstudy 1999" (1999), at www.corp.aol.com/press/study/youthstudy.pdf.

21. See D. Finkelhor, K. J. Mitchell, and J. Wolak, *Online Victimization: A Report on the Nation's Youth* (2000), Crimes Against Children Research Centre, at www.missingkids.com.

22. "Child Abuse and the Internet," *Child Abuse Prevention Issues*, no. 15 (Summer 2001), National Child Protection Clearinghouse, www.aifs.org.au/nch/issues15.html. This excellent article pointed to most of the references in this section of the book.

23. See J. Carr, "An Innocent Encounter," *Professional Social Work* (July 2001): 12-13.

24. See Starch, "American Online Cyberstudy."

25. See Finkelhor, Mitchell, and Wolak, *Online Victimization*.

26. That is, provide tourists with a listing and description of children available for sex. See *Childright*, no. 133 (UK: Children's Legal Centre, 1997); and H. Sellier, "The World Citizens' Movement to Protect Innocence in Danger," in *Child Abuse on the Internet: Ending the Silence*, ed. Carlos A. Arnaldo (Paris: Berghahn Books and UNESCO, 2001), 173-75.

27. See Sellier, "World Citizens' Movement."

28. T. Costello, "Gambling's Great Web of Lies," *The Age* 3 (April 2001): 15.

29. See S. Wellard, "Cause and Effect," *Community Care*, vol. 15 (March 2001): 26-27.

30. John R. Levine, Carol Baroudi, and Margaret Levine Young, *The Internet for Dummies* (New York: Hungry Minds Inc. 2002), 253.

31. See www.prevent-abuse-now.com/law2ac.html.

32. The text of this declaration and action plan can be found at: www.unesco.org/webworld/child_screen/conf_index.html.

33. See www.innocenceendanger.org/innocence/about_innocence.html.

CHAPTER 2. MYTHS AND FACTS ABOUT SEXUAL ABUSE AND SEX OFFENDERS

1. Contrasting 1 Corinthians 7:8 ("To the unmarried and the widows I say that it is well for them to remain unmarried as I am") with 1 Timothy 4:4 ("For everything created by God is good, and nothing is to be rejected") denies a prohibition against marriage, among other practices.

2. Specific references for these organizations are intentionally not provided.

3. Mildred Daley Pagelow, *Family Violence* (New York: Praeger, 1984), 3.

4. Sandra L. Bloom, "Psychodynamics of Preventing Child Abuse," *The Journal of Psychohistory* 21, no. 1 (1993): 53-67.

5. *The Inquirer Sunday Review*, Section C, p. 1.

6. Kim Oates, *The Spectrum of Child Abuse: Assessment, Treatment, and Prevention* (New York: Brunner/Mazel, 1996). On p. 95 of *Spectrum of Child Abuse*, Oates cites C. Matthews, *Breaking Through* (London: Lion Press, 1990).

7. Daniel L. Schacter, *Searching for Memory: The Brain, the Mind, and the Past* (New York: Basic Books, 1996), 273.

8. See my previously cited doctoral dissertation, "Engaging Neighborhoods: A Neighborhood-based Strategy for the Primary Prevention of Child Maltreatment in the United States."

9. *Parade, Philadelphia Enquirer* (14 July 2002): 4-5.

10. M. Scott Peck, *People of the Lie: The Hope for Healing Human Evil* (New York: Simon & Schuster, 1983).

11. Barry Glassner, *The Culture of Fear: Why Americans Are Afraid of the Wrong Things* (New York: Basic Books, 1999), 40.

12. Robert Thornton, "Prevention and the Roman Catholic Clergy" (Psy.D. dissertation, Widener University, 1995), 7.

13. See G. Gabbard's essay "Psychotherapists Who Transgress Sexual Boundaries with Patients," in *The Breach of Trust: Sexual Exploitation by Health Care Professionals and Clergy*, ed. John C. Gonsiorek (Thousand Oaks, Calif.: Sage Publications, 1995).

14. This is my summary of R. Irons's essay "The Sexually Exploitive Professional." Monograph, Second Conference on Addiction: Prevention, Recognition, and Treatment. Baltimore, Md.: Behavioral Care Network/Abbott Northwestern Hospital.

15. See M. Laaser, "Sexual Addiction and the Clergy," in *Pastoral Psychology* 39, no. 4 (1991): 213-35.

16. A more complete discussion of assessment of recidivism risk can be found in "Taking Risks: How Psychological Assessment Can Drive Treatment Planning for Persons with Mental Illness or Mental Retardation Who Engage in Sex Offending Behaviors," previously presented by me at the 2002 Midwinter Conference of the Society for Personality Assessment.

17. Robert Hare provides an excellent and accessible description of psychopaths in *Without Conscience: The Disturbing World of Psychopaths among Us* (New York: Guilford Press, 1999). The symptoms cited are taken from his discussion on p. 34.

18. T. Millon, E. Simonsen, M. Birket-Smith, and R. D. Davis, eds., *Psychopathy: Antisocial, Criminal, and Violent Behavior* (New York: Guilford Press, 1998), 304.

19. Robert Hare, in *Psychopathy*, 200-201.

20. Hare, *Without Conscience*, 93.

21. Ibid., 205-6.

CHAPTER 3. SOME SOLUTIONS: PREVENTION AND RESPONSE

1. These figures are based upon year 2000 data from www.infoplease.com; from www.whitehouse.gov/fsbr/crime.html (Social Statistics Briefing Room); and www.cdc.gov/nchs/default.html (National Center for Health Statistics).

2. Ideas regarding the violation of covenant are related to work by Marie Fortune (See *Violence in the Family* [Cleveland: Pilgrim Press, 1991]), and notions of "creating sanctuary" are attributed in part to the book *Creating Sanctuary: Toward the Evolution of Sane Societies* by Dr. Sandra L. Bloom (New York: Routledge, 1997).

3. One chapter of the *Boston Globe*'s 2002 exposé entitled *Betrayal* cites the Lafayette diocese's secret payment of $4.2 million to nine victims of one priest and another chapter reported that the Archdiocese of Boston quietly settled allegations against 70 priests over a ten-year period for an undisclosed amount of money (Boston: Little, Brown, 2002).

4. Ibid.

5. Jason Berry, *Lead Us Not into Temptation: Catholic Priests and the Sexual Abuse of Children* (New York: Doubleday, 1992).

6. Drawn from *Child Abuse and Neglect: Critical First Steps in Response to a National Emergency* (Washington, D.C.: Advisory Board on Child Abuse and Neglect, 1990) and quoted in *Creating Caring Communities: Blueprint for an Effective Federal Policy on Child Abuse and Neglect* (Washington, D.C.: U.S. Advisory Board on Child Abuse and Neglect, 1991), 61.

7. A further discussion of risk is available in my article *Taking Risks: How Psychological Assessment Can Drive Treatment Planning for Persons with Mental Illness or Mental Retardation Who Engage in Sex Offending Behaviors* presented at the 2001 Midwinter conference of the Society of Personality Assessment

8. The Psychological Assessment Work Group published an excellent (but detailed) article highlighting the validity of psychological tests and distinguishing testing from assessment ("Psychological Testing and Psychological Assessment: A Review of Evidence and Issues," *American Psychologist* 56 [2001]: 128-65).

9. For this reason, the best current assessments used to determine the likelihood of a past offender to reoffend are based largely on specific aspects and frequency of past sex-offending behavior. (See *Static-99: Improving Actuarial Risk Assessments for Sex Offenders,* user report 99-02 [Ottawa: Department of the Solicitor General of Canada, 1999]; and *The Sex Offender Need Assessment Rating (SONAR): A Method for Measuring Change in Risk Levels,* user report 00-01 [Ottawa: Department of the Solicitor General of Canada, 2000].)

10. In Pennsylvania, the Pennsylvania State Police Request for Criminal Record Check (SP4-164) and the Pennsylvania Child Abuse History Clearance (CY113) are examples of background checks.

11. While good, bad, and confusing touch has not been seen in print by the author, a handout from the Family Support Line of Delaware County lists these three and cites The Center for the Prevention of Sexual and Domestic Violence (Marie Fortune's Washington state organization) as its source.

12. These questions are likewise credited to The Center for the Prevention of Sexual and Domestic Violence (1992) by the Family Support Line of Delaware County Inc.

13. In Pennsylvania at this writing, for example, conviction of a first offense of nonreporting is a summary offense with a maximum penalty of a $300 fine and/or ninety days in jail. Subsequent convictions are misdemeanors of the third degree with a maximum penalty of $2500 and/or one year in jail.

14. Although clinical experience bears out these predictable responses, they are also well described in Marie Fortune's *Violence in the Family*.

15. The New Jersey Department of Human Services; Division of Youth and Family Services (1995) report entitled *Children at Risk, 1993 and 1994,* for example, uses these designations for the disposition of allegations.

16. One could request a copy of "Sexual Misconduct Policies and Procedure," an excellent document from the Presbytery of Philadelphia whose E-mail address is available from their web site.

CHAPTER 4. UNDERSTANDING VICTIMS

1. D. A. Sexton, D. Tarter, and K. Gunn, *Healing the Wounds of Childhood: The Resource Guide for Adult Survivors of Childhood Abuse and Addiction* (Scottsdale, Ariz., Childhelp U.S.A., 1992). National Survivors of Child Abuse and Addictions Program and Childhelp IOF Foresters Hotline (1-800-4-A-CHILD), the nation's largest child abuse prevention hotline (according to this publication). P.O. Box 630, Hollywood, CA 90028.

2. In my dissertation, "Engaging Neighborhoods," thirty-three empirical studies are cited, documenting the long-term effects of physical child abuse. That compilation was representative, but not exhaustive. On the other hand, there continues to be a paucity of empirically based documentation regarding the long-term effects of child sexual abuse. I suspect that funding for prevention programs aimed at physical child abuse required the foregoing studies and that those prevention efforts served to help prevent all forms of child abuse, so studies specific to child sexual abuse were not immediately needed.

3. Debatably, Joseph did, however, narrowly escape an experience of sexual abuse at the hands of Potiphar's wife.

4. James Leehan, *Pastoral Care for Survivors of Family Abuse* (Louisville, Ky.: Westminster/John Knox Press, 1989).

CHAPTER 5. MINISTRY WITH VICTIMS, ABUSERS, AND THEIR FAMILIES

1. From "Elders and Sexual Abuse—A Pastor's Dilemma" published in *Ordained Servant* 11, no. 4 (2002).

2. One might point out that the command in Matthew 18:22 to forgive seventy times seven follows immediately after the discussion of confronting the sinner with the sin (Matt. 18:15-20).

3. Note that Paul's counsel for wives to be subject to their husbands (Eph. 4:22) is not separate from his direction for husbands to love their wives (Eph. 4:25). Husbands do not love their wives when they either rape them or abuse their children. Indeed, Paul speaks of "mutual submission" rather than a "one way" submission in the very next chapter (Eph. 5:21).

4. Especially for those who understand "discipline" to mean "teaching," the child sexual abuser who believes he or she is "training" the child forgets that Proverbs 22:6 admonishes the training of children "in the right way" or "in the way that they should go." Sexual abuse is not the "right way."

5. Although Romans 12:12 urges "patience in suffering," it does not necessarily imply silence, and one may well infer that Paul intends us to patiently bear the suffering that is connected with our faith in the gospel, not the suffering of abuse. One might also note that Paul also said: "If one member suffers, all suffer together" (1 Cor. 12:26).

6. From an e-mail from Dr. Dan Bagby to me, dated Wednesday, January 22, 2003.

7. Garret Keizer, *The Enigma of Anger: Essays on a Sometimes Deadly Sin* (San Francisco: Jossey-Bass, 2002). Dr. Dan Bagby (this book's editor) notes that he likewise has written on "anger as care" in the chapter "Tears of Anger" in *Seeing Through Our Tears: Why We Cry, How We Heal* (Minneapolis: Augsburg Press, 1999), and earlier in *Understanding Anger in the Church* (Nashville: Broadman Press, 1979, out of print).

8. Keizer, *Enigma of Anger,* 129.

9. "Elders and Sexual Abuse," 75.

10. The reporting information here, as well as additional news and resources to help in case of any child abuse (physical or sexual), can be found at www.childhelp.org.

EPILOGUE: SEXUAL SHALOM

1. Available only on CD-ROM, the book is *Shalom: A Study of the Biblical Concept of Peace* by Donald E. Gowan (Pittsburgh: The Kerygma Program Inc., 2002).

2. Marva J. Dawn, *Sexual Character: Beyond Technique to Intimacy* (Grand Rapids, Mich.: Eerdmans, 1993).

3. As discussed in the Shalom study referenced above.

4. Nancy Myer Hopkins, "The Congregation Is Also a Victim," Special Papers and Research Reports (Washington, D.C.: Alban Institute, 1994).

5. See Edwin, H. Friedman, *Generation to Generation: Family Process in Church and Synagogue* (New York: Guilford Press, 1985).

6. According to Darlene Haskin, in her chapter "Afterpastors in Troubled Congregations" in *Restoring the Soul of a Church: Healing Congregations Wounded by Clergy Sexual Misconduct,* ed. Nancy Myer Hopkins and Mark Laaser (Collegeville, Minn.: Liturgical Press, 1995), the term was coined by the pastors who, themselves, succeeded clergy abusers (p. 155).

7. For example: Hopkins and Laaser, *Restoring the Soul of a Church,* and Nils Friberg, "A Denominational Survival Kit for Afterpastors," and "Clergy Sexual Misconduct: A Systems Perspective," ed. Nancy Myer Hopkins (Washington, D.C.: Alban Institute, 1993).